BLUES
GUITAR
BIBLE

This publication is not authorised for sale in the
United States of America and/or Canada.

Hal Leonard Europe
Distributed by Music Sales

Exclusive Distributors:
Music Sales Limited
8/9 Frith Street, London W1D 3JB, England.
Music Sales Pty Limited
120 Rothschild Avenue, Rosebery, NSW 2018, Australia.

Order No. HLE90001553
ISBN 0-7119-8735-1
This book © Copyright 2001 by Hal Leonard Europe

Printed in the USA
Cover design by Chloë Alexander

Your Guarantee of Quality
As publishers, we strive to produce every book to the highest
commercial standards.
The book has been carefully designed to minimise awkward page
turns and to make playing from it a real pleasure.
Throughout, the printing and binding have been planned to ensure a
sturdy, attractive publication which should give years of enjoyment.
If your copy fails to meet our high standards, please inform us and
we will gladly replace it.

Music Sales' complete catalogue describes thousands of titles and is
available in full colour sections by subject, direct from
Music Sales Limited. Please state your areas of interest and send a
cheque/postal order for £1.50 for postage to: Music Sales Limited,
Newmarket Road, Bury St. Edmunds, Suffolk IP33 3YB, England.

www.musicsales.com

CONTENTS

All Your Love (I Miss Loving)

Words and Music by Otis Rush

*Gtr. 1 plays w/ triplet feel (♫ = ♪³♪) till indicated. ** Chords symbols reflect overall tonality.

***Gtr. 1 plays w/ straight eighths feel (♫ = ♫) till indicated.

Verse

1. All the love I miss lov-in',
all the kiss-es I miss kiss-in'.
ba - by,
I have in store for you. —

simile on repeat

Rhy. Fig. 1

All the love I miss lov-in', ____
All the love, pret - ty ba - by, ____
all the kiss-es I miss
I have in store for

kiss - in'. __
you. _____

Be - fore I met you, ba - by,
The way I love you, ba - by,

End Rhy. Fig. 1

I did - n't know what I was miss - in'. _____

2. All the love, _____ pret - ty

*Gtr. 1 plays w/ triplet feel ( ) till Outro.

Interlude

Gtr. 2 tacet

7

*Played slightly behind the beat.

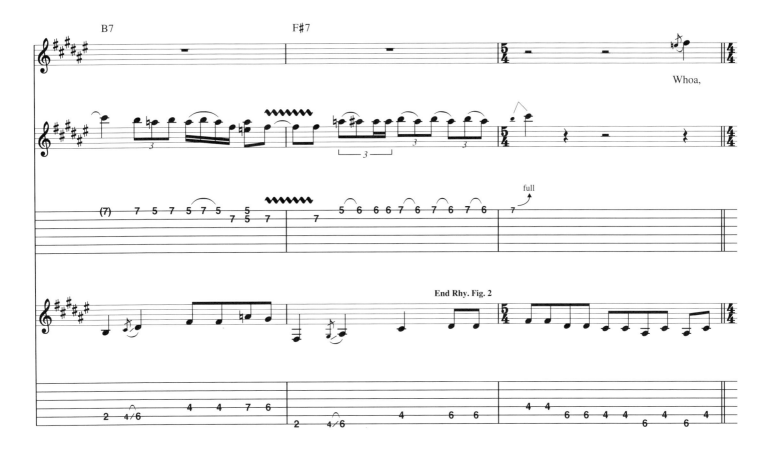

Chorus

whoa, whoa, ba - by.   You know I love you, ba - by. ___   Yeah, ___

___ yeah, ___ ba - by. _____   You know I love you, ba - by. ___   I ___

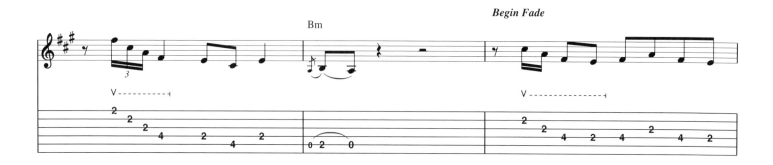

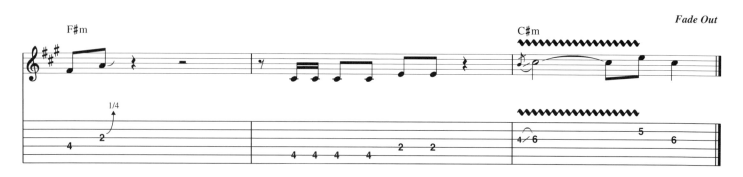

Better Off With the Blues

Words and Music by Gary Nicholson, Donnie Fritts and Delbert McClinton

It may sound fun-ny, but it's   true: _
And it's   the   less of two   evils:

I think I'm bet-ter off   with the

blues.

Guitar Solo

Blue on Black

Words and Music by Tia Sillers, Mark Selby and Kenny Wayne Shepherd

Gtr. 1: w/ Rhy. Fig. 1, 2 times, simile
Gtr. 3: w/ Riff A1, 2 times, simile

* Set to harmonize one octave above.

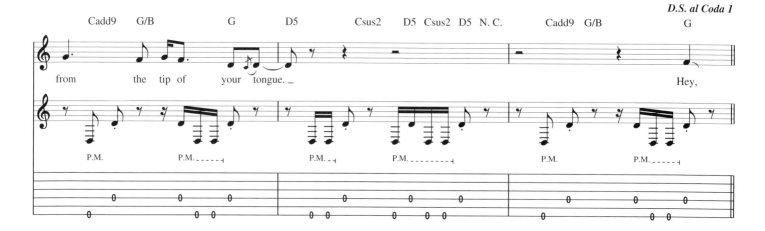

from the tip of your tongue. _ Hey,

⊕ *Coda 1*

Gtr. 1: w/ Rhy. Fig. 1, 2 times, simile
Gtr. 3: w/ Riff A1, 2 times, simile

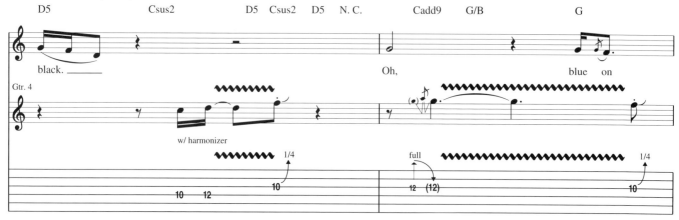

black. _____ Oh, blue on

w/ harmonizer

black. Oh, yeah. _____

Guitar Solo

Gtr. 1: w/ Rhy. Fig.1, 6 times, simile
Gtr. 3: w/ Riff A1, 6 times, simile

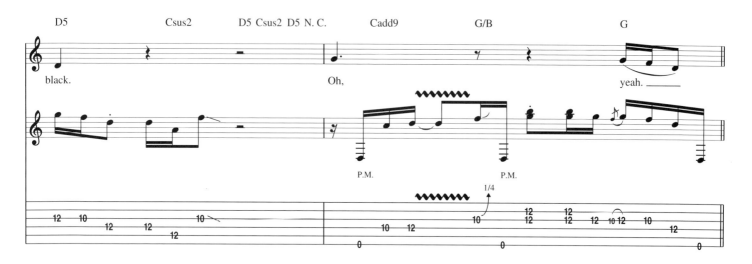

rake

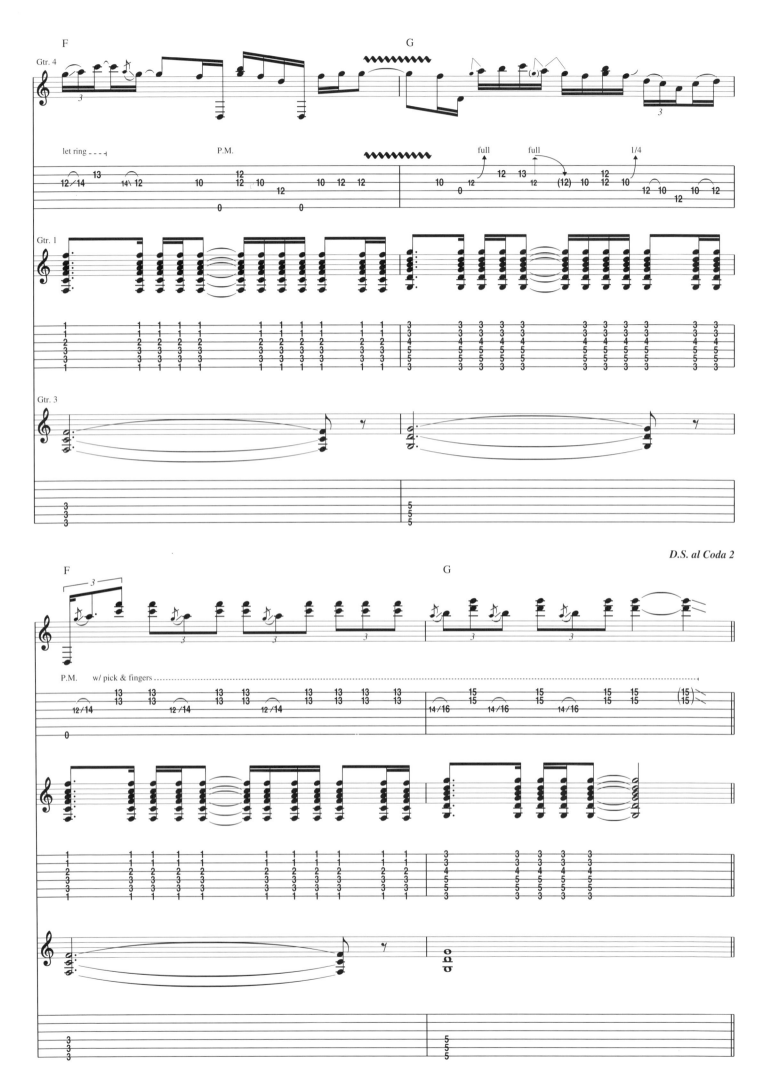

D.S. al Coda 2

Bo Diddley

Words and Music by Ellas McDaniel

Guitar Solo

f

let chords ring

semi-mute -

2nd Verse

2. Bo — Did - dle-y caught a   nan-ny   goat _____   to

simile

- ┤ cont. semi-muting

make his pret-ty ba- by a   Sun - day coat.

Bo Did-dle-y caught a bear - cat, __ to

make his pret-ty ba- by a Sun - day hat. __

Guitar Solo

semi-mute

semi-mute

(A9)   (G)

semi-mute

semi-mute

let chords ring

C   Eb   C

G

semi-mute

C

D(add4) C

G

Let chords ring

semi-mute

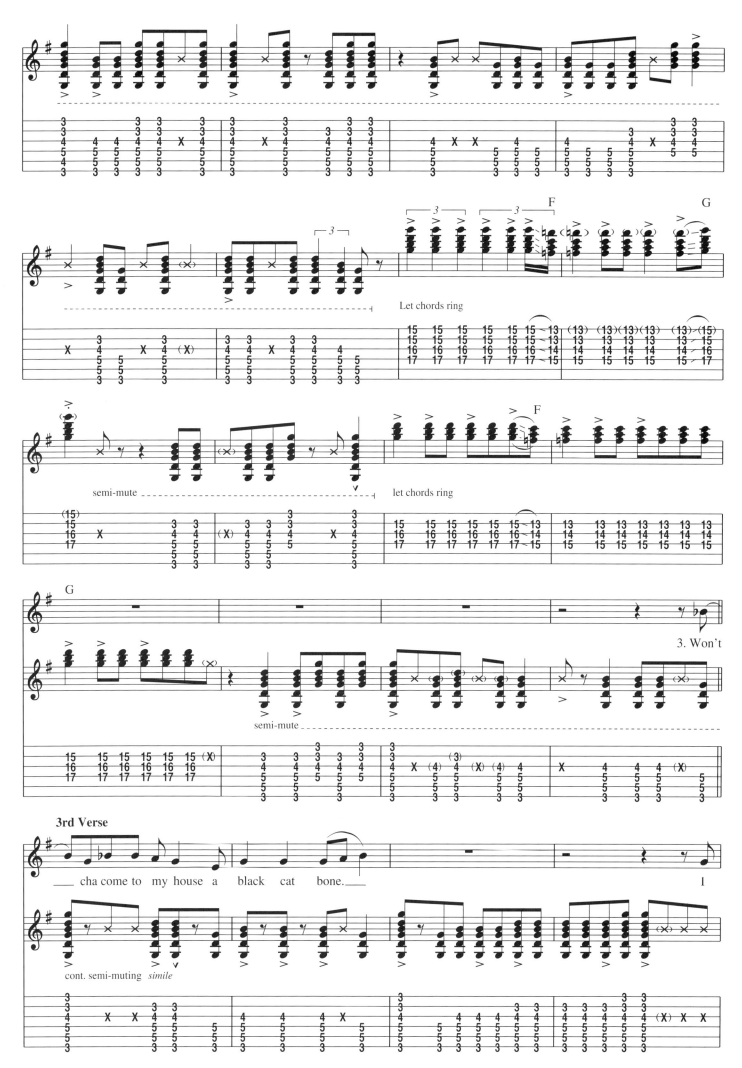

3rd Verse

___ cha come to my house a black cat bone.___

cont. semi-muting *simile*

take my ba-by a - way from home.

Cov-er that mo-jo an' where's he been?

up yo' house 'n' gone a - gain.

Bo Did - dle-y, Bo Did-dle-y,

have you heard?_____ My_

___ pur - ty ba - by that she was mur-der-ed

Guitar Solo

(G#)   (G)

semi-muted

(Gb)   (G)

semi-muted

semi-muted

Gsus4   G

semi-muted

F# G   E   F   G   *Fade Out*

Cincinnati Jail

Words and Music by Lonnie Mack

† Gtr. 1: Tune Down 1 Step, Capo V

① = D   ④ = C
② = A   ⑤ = G
③ = F   ⑥ = D

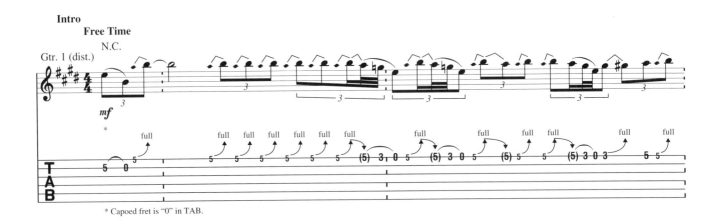

* Capoed fret is "0" in TAB.

** Symbols above reflect actual sounding chord.

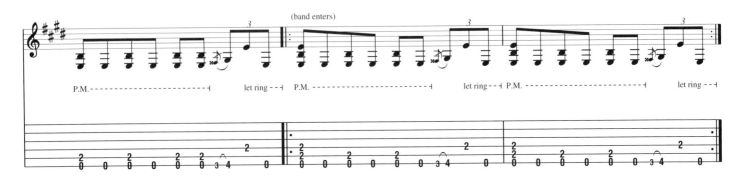

† Editors Note: You can accomplish the same result without tuning down
a whole step by remaining in standard tuning and capoing the third fret.

Guitar Solo

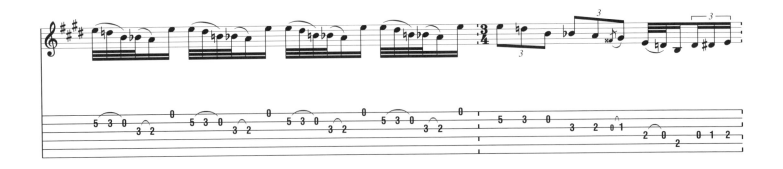

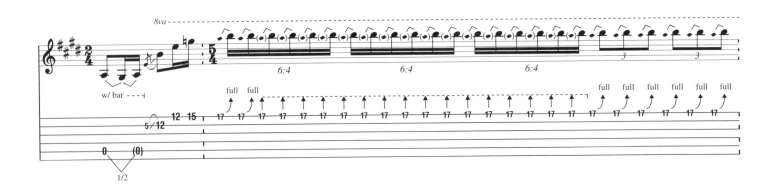

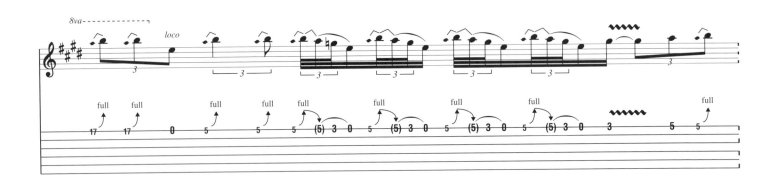

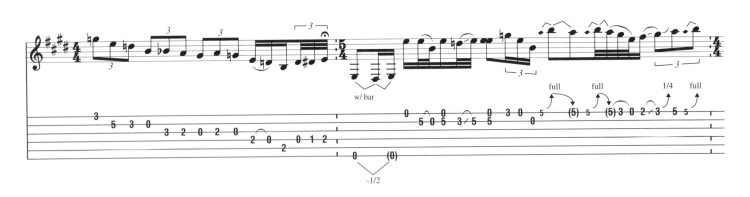

Collins Mix

By Albert Collins

Em Tuning, Capo VIII

④ –E ① –E

⑤ –B ② –B

⑥ –E ③ –G

Medium Shuffle ♩ = 130

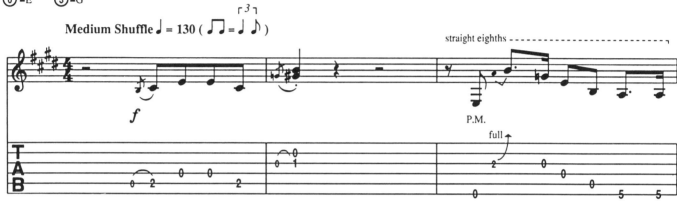

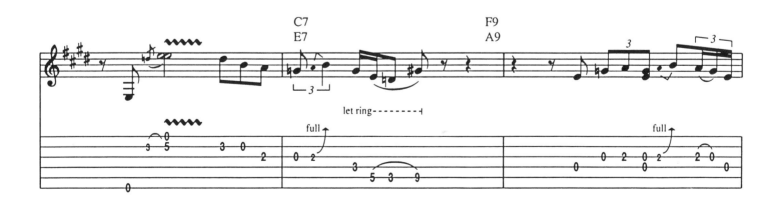

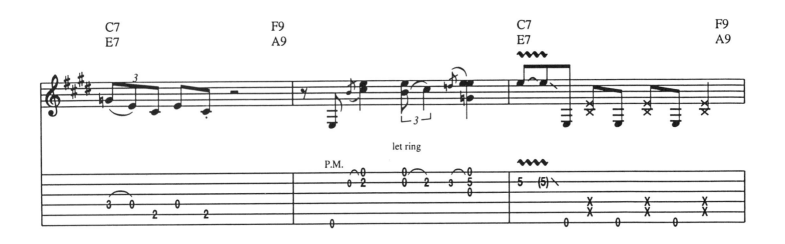

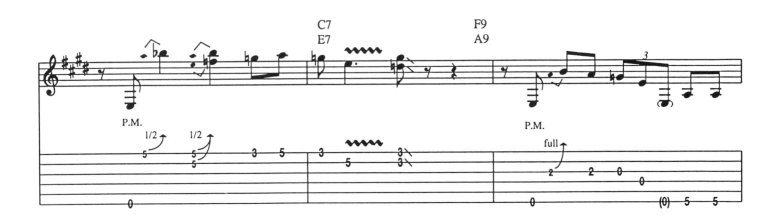

Don't Throw Your Love on Me So Strong

Words and Music by Albert King

Tune down 1 step:
(low to high) D–G–C–F–A–D

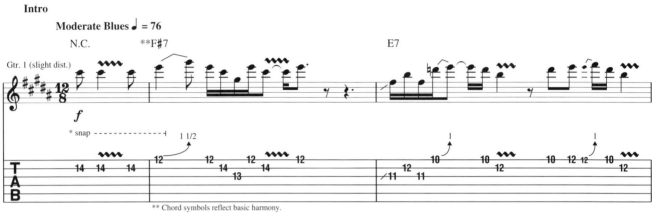

** Chord symbols reflect basic harmony.

* Snap string with index finger.

ba-by,   don't throw your love on me   so strong. _____

Yeah, _ your love is like _ a fau - cet. _   You can turn it off ___ and on. _

Verse

2. Hey,   ba - by,

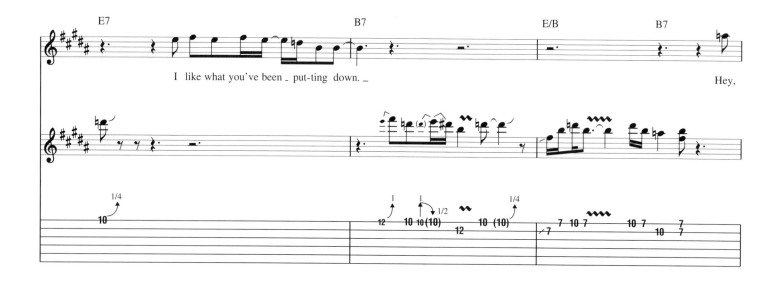

I like what you've been _ put-ting down. _

Hey,

ba - by,

I like what you've been put-ting down.

Oh, but you can _ search the whole _ world o - ver _

and no love like yours _ can be

found. ___

Ah. ___

3. And ___ some-day ba-by,

Verse

Everyday (I Have the Blues)

Words and Music by Peter Chatman

* Chord symbols reflect overall tonality throughout.

* Played behind the beat.

Hide Away

Words and Music by Freddie King and Sonny Thompson

* Chord symbols reflect overall tonality.

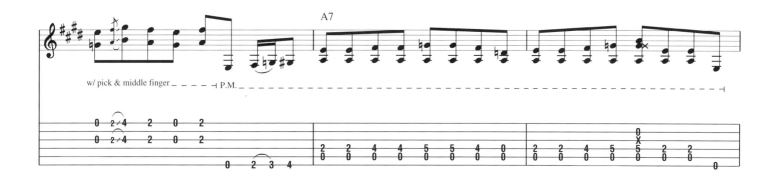

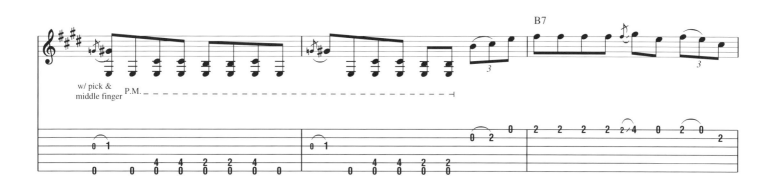

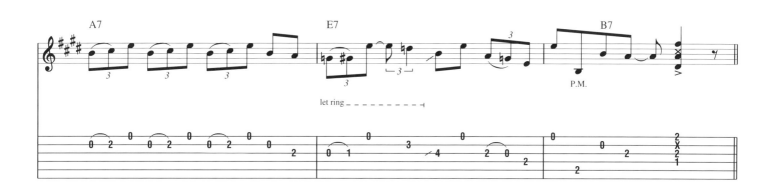

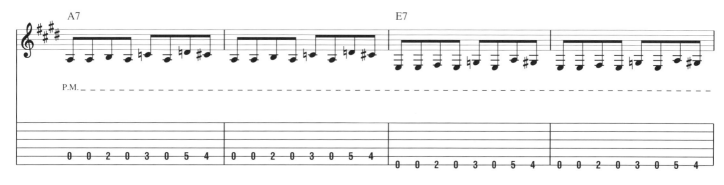

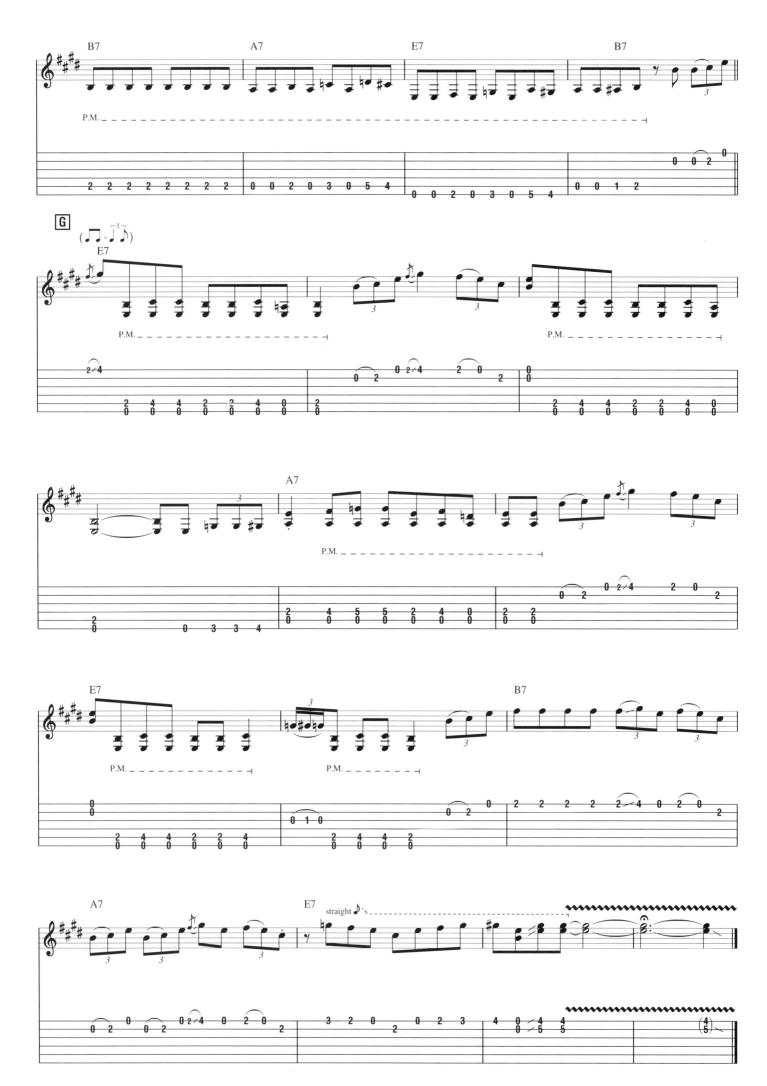

I Smell a Rat

By Buddy Guy

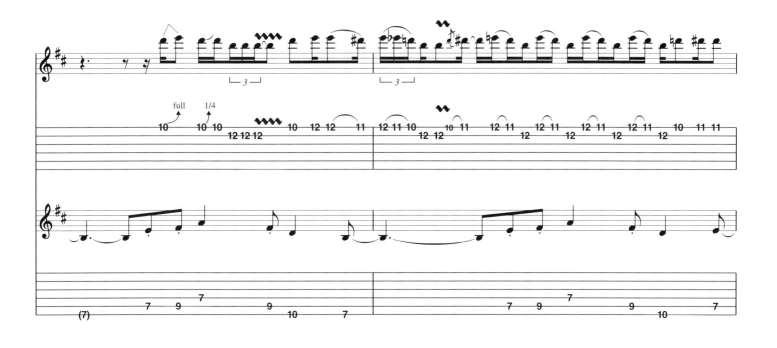

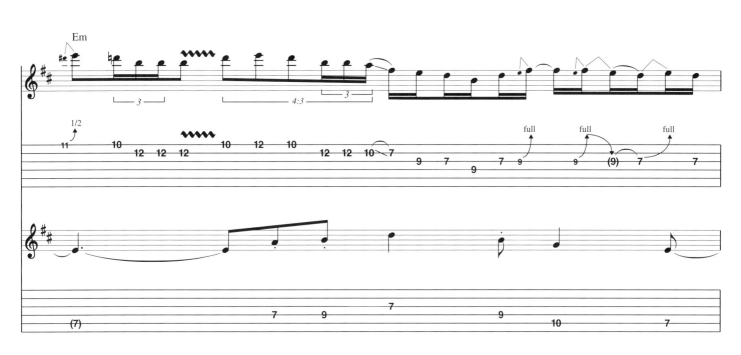

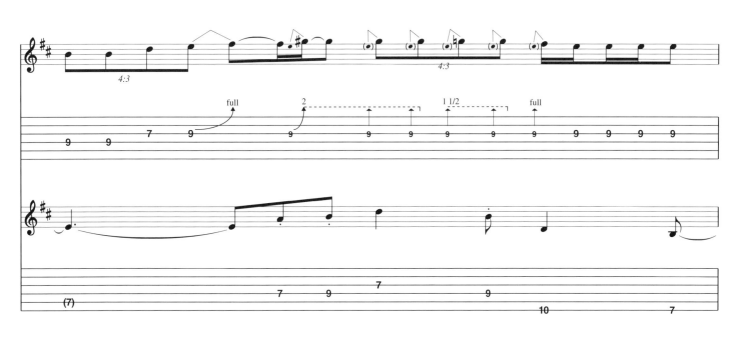

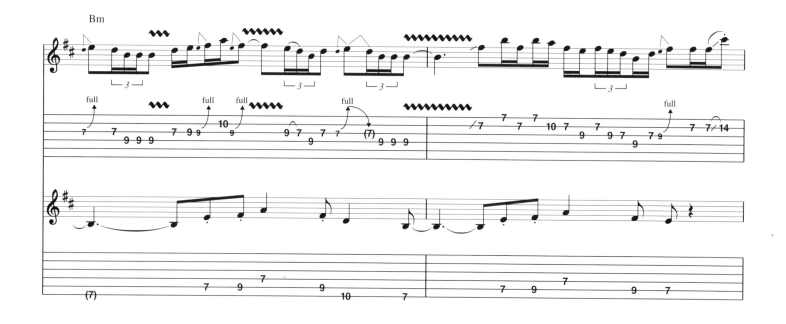

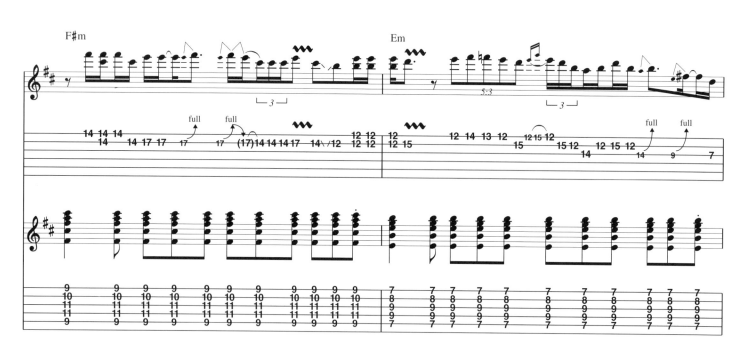

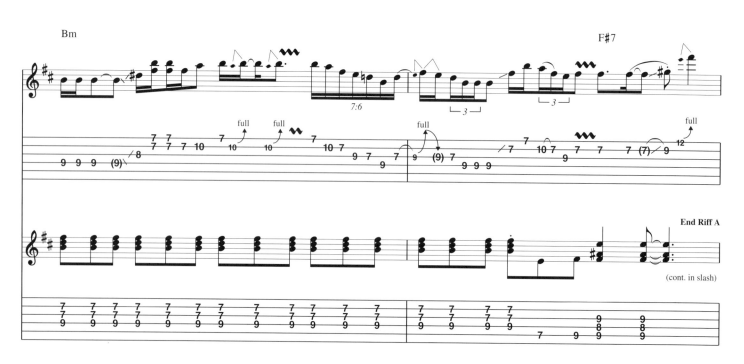

Spoken: Ho, c'mon fellas now!

*1st note is struck, not tied.

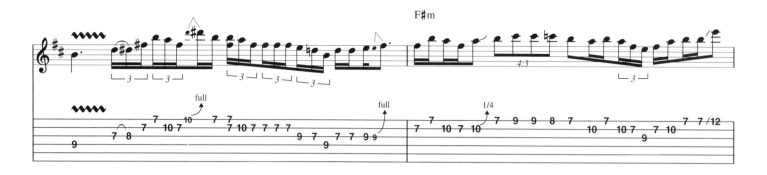

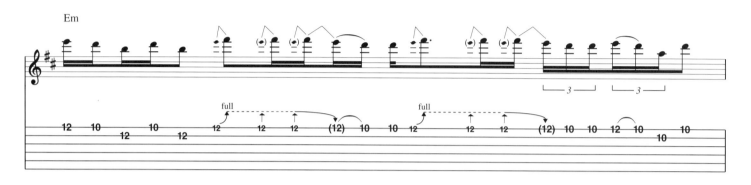

Verse

Gtr. 1 tacet

1. I think I smell a rat in my house, __ hon-ey.

Ba-by, I be-lieve he got just two legs, _____ ha, ha, yes. Oh,

(cont. in notation)

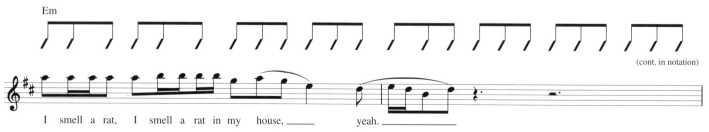

I smell a rat, I smell a rat in my house, _____ yeah. _____

Hon - ey, I think he walk - in' 'round   on   two   legs. ____

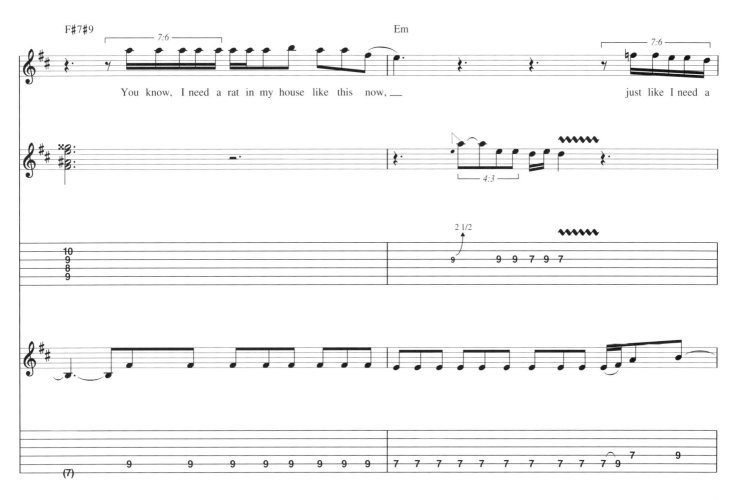

You know, I need a rat in my house like this   now, ___   just like I need a

*T = Thumb on ⑥.

Verse

Gtr. 1 tacet
Gtr. 2: w/ Rhy. Fig. 1, 1st time, simile
Gtr. 2: w/ Riff A, 2nd & 3rd times, simile

2. You claim to be a-fraid at night.
3. You got my back door wide o-pen.
4. *See Additional Lyrics*

You said you can't stay home all a-lone, ___
Bab-y you say you s'posed to be a-fraid. ___

Uh, huh, yes.
Oh, ___ you said you're
Oh, ___ you

'fraid, ___ you're 'fraid to stay home at night.
got my back door wide o-pen, ___ ha, ha.

You said you did-n't

Gtr. 2: w/ *Riff A, last 6 meas., 1st time, simile
Gtr. 1: w/ Fill 1, 3rd time
N.C.(Bm)

wan-na be home a-lone. ___
And you tell me sup-posed to be a-fraid. _____

Oh,

Fill 1
Gtr. 1

mf

62

but I keep smell-in' that rat ev-'ry time I get back _ and, and all, and all you do is wan-na make me
ha, ha. You know the last time I slept with it o-pen, _ you know in Chi-ca-go, I al-most lost my

1.

moan. _____

Gtr. 1

2.

head. _____

Gtr. 1

3.

go, _____ I can be found. _

Gtr. 1

Guitar Solo

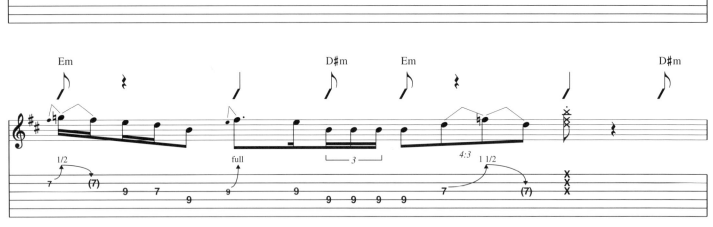

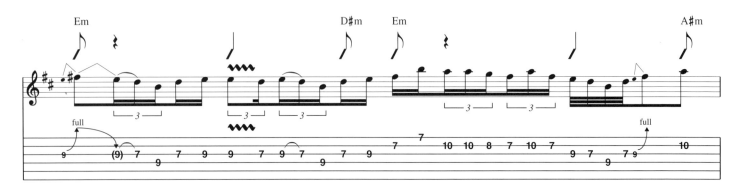

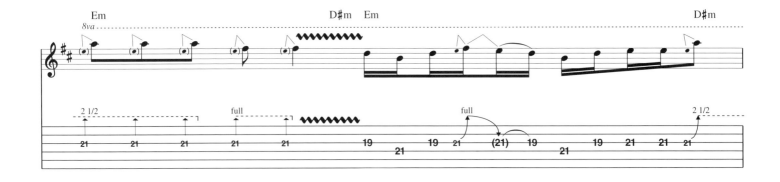

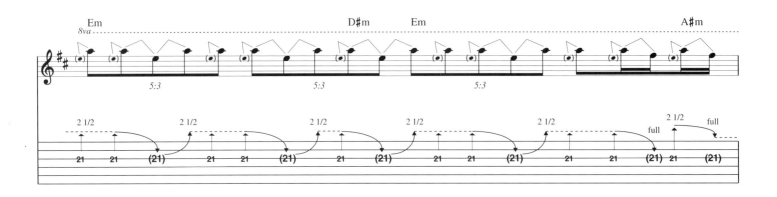

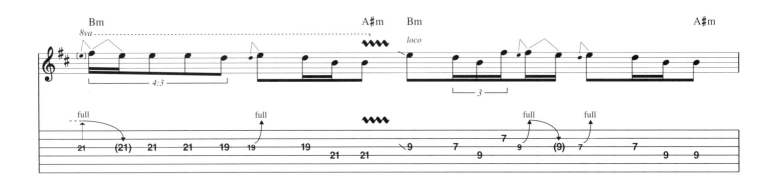

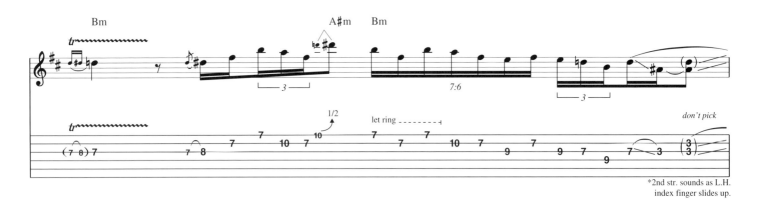

*2nd str. sounds as L.H.
index finger slides up.

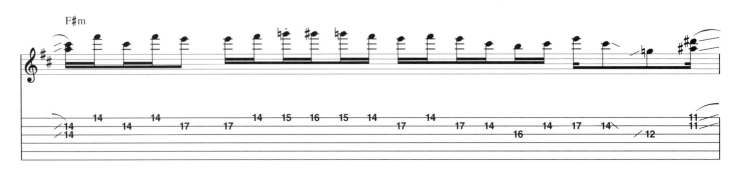

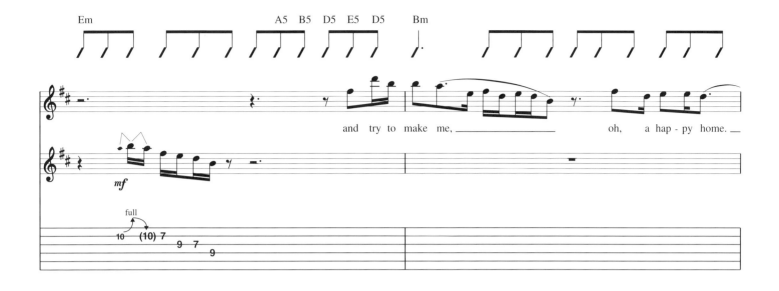

and try to make me, _____ oh, a hap-py home. ___

Outro-Guitar Solo

w/ ad lib. Voc.

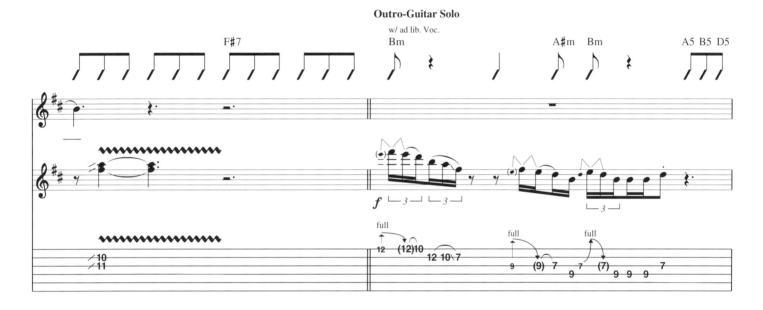

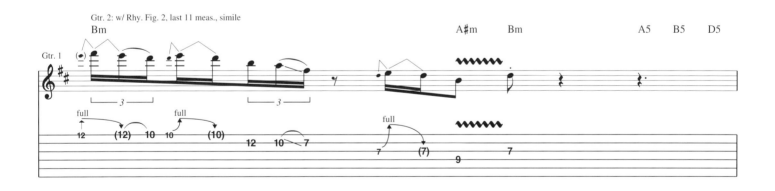

Gtr. 2: w/ Rhy. Fig. 2, last 11 meas., simile

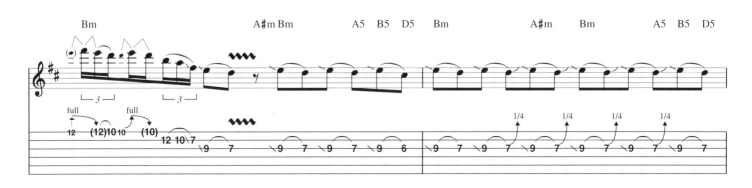

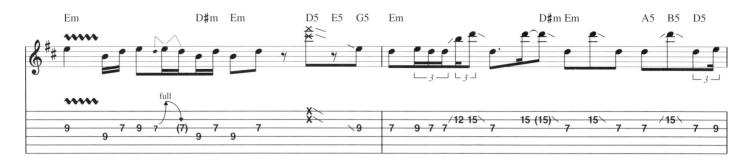
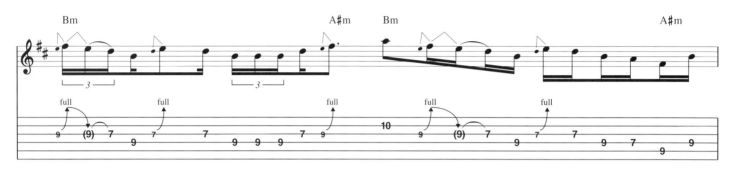
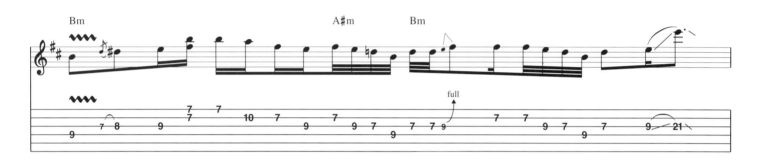
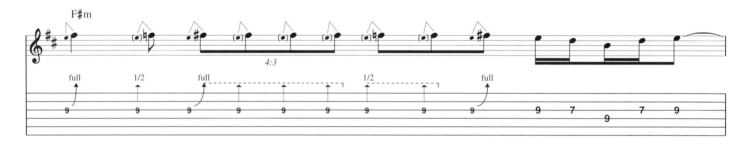
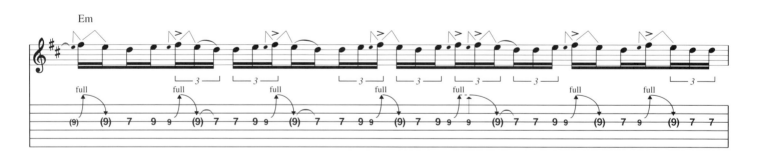
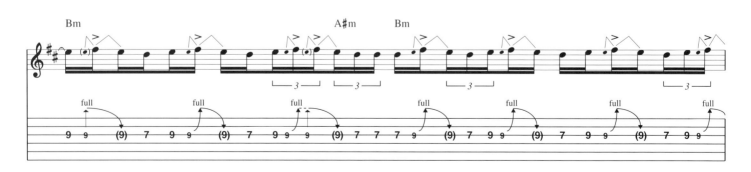

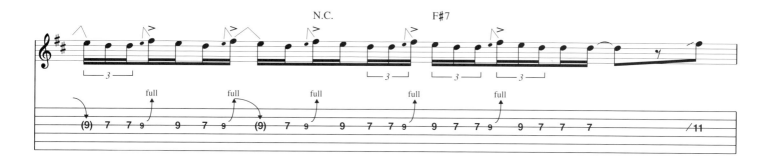

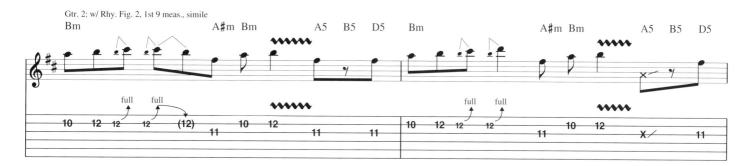

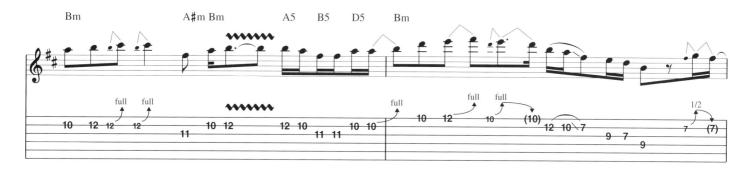

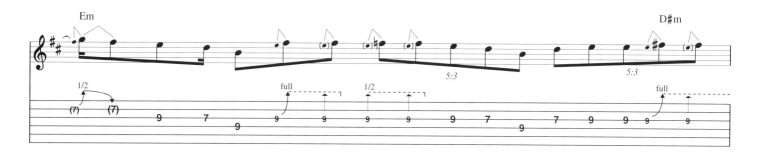

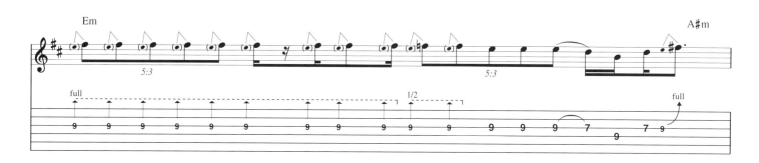

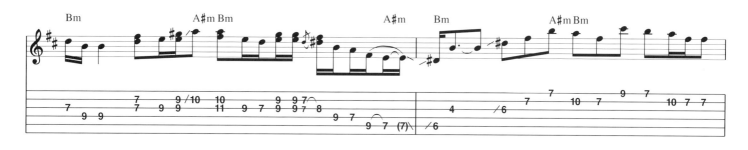

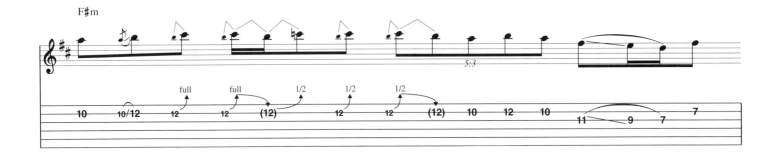

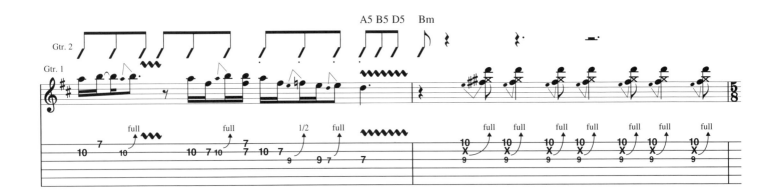

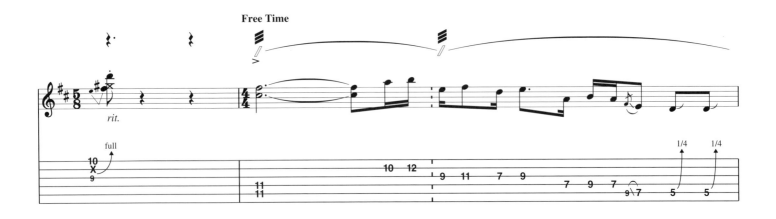

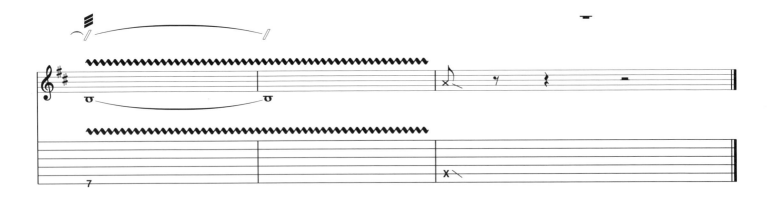

Additional Lyrics

4. Sometime I think you're foolin' me, baby.
   And I do believe you're just jivin' me around.
   Spoken: You better stop that.
   Oh, sometime I think you're foolin' me, baby, ha, ha. Uh huh,
   Honey, I think you're just jivin' me around.
   Why don't you leave me or not woman?
   You know, I think there's another woman,
   I can go, I can be found.

I'm Tore Down

Words and Music by Sonny Thompson

* Chord symbols reflect suggested tonality.

Chorus

tore down, al - most lev - el with the ground. Why'd __ I

Gtr. 1

feel __ like this __ when __ my ba - by can't be found? 2. I

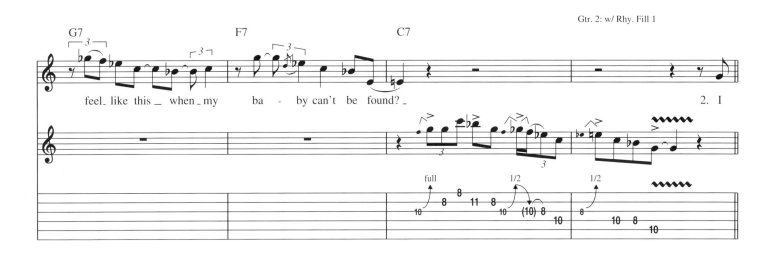

Gtr. 2: w/ Rhy. Fill 1

𝄉 Verse

love you babe __ with all my heart __ and soul. __ Love like mine __ will nev - er grow old.

3. Love you ba - by with all __ my might. __ Love like mine __ is out - ta sight. I'll

Gtrs. 1 & 2

Rhy. Fill 1
Gtr. 2

Love you in the morn-ing and in the eve - ning too. _ Ev-'ry time you leave me I get mad_ with you. _ Well, I'm
lie for you _____ if you want me to. _ I real - ly don't be - lieve that your _ love is true. Well, I'm

Chorus

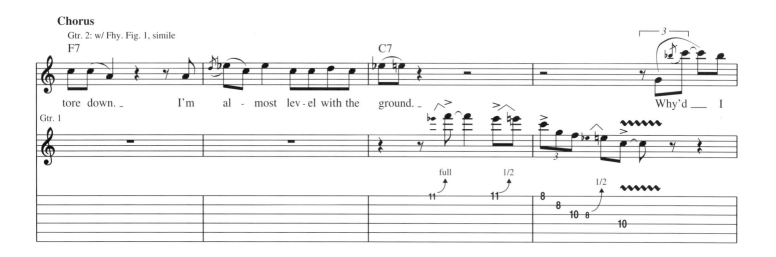

tore down. _ I'm al - most lev - el with the ground. _ Why'd __ I

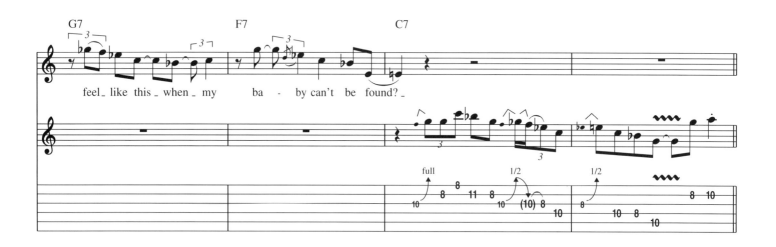

feel_ like this _ when _ my ba - by can't be found? _

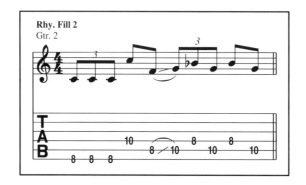

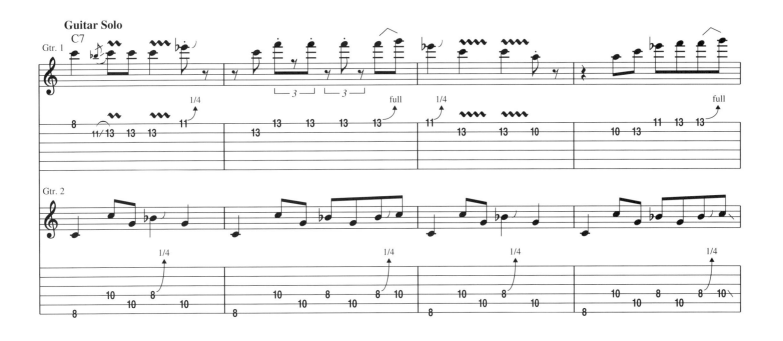

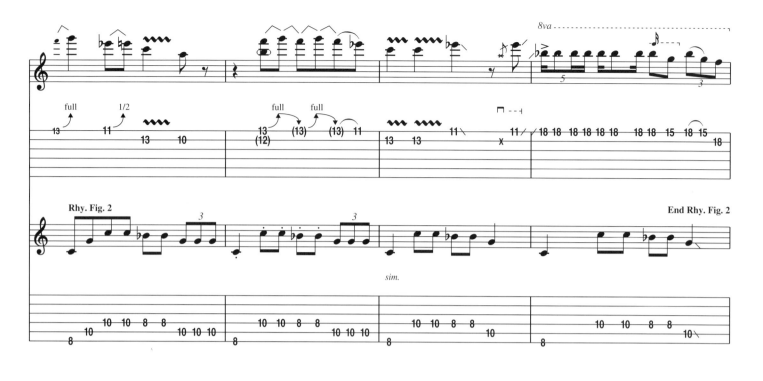

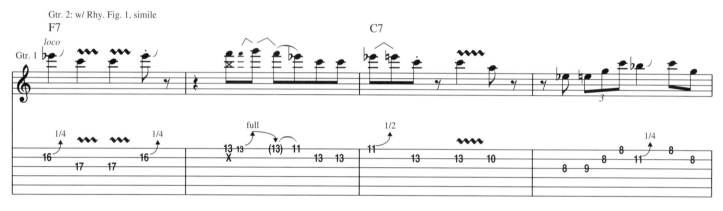

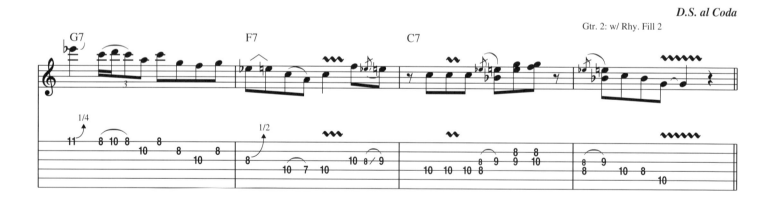

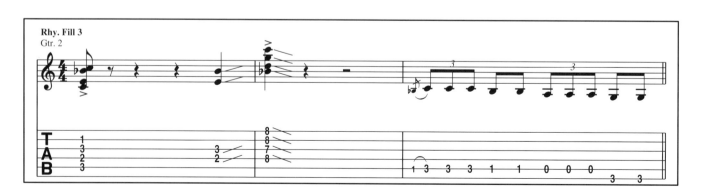

Coda

Chorus

Gtr. 2: w/ Rhy. Fig. 1, simile

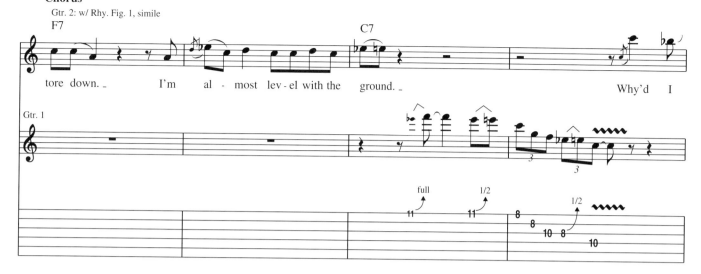

tore down. _ I'm al - most lev - el with the ground. _ Why'd I

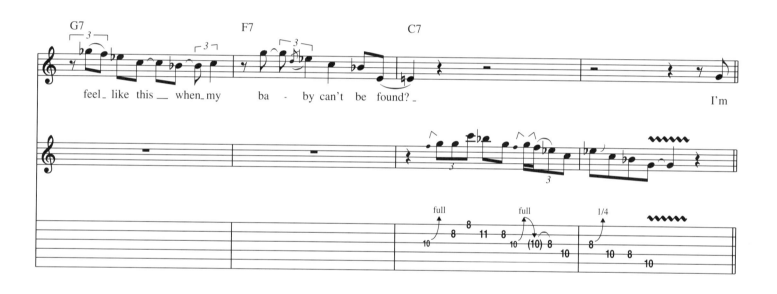

feel _ like this _ when _ my ba - by can't be found? _ I'm

Out-Chorus

Gtr. 2: w/ Rhy. Fig. 2, simile

tore down _ al - most lev - el with the ground. _ Well, I'm

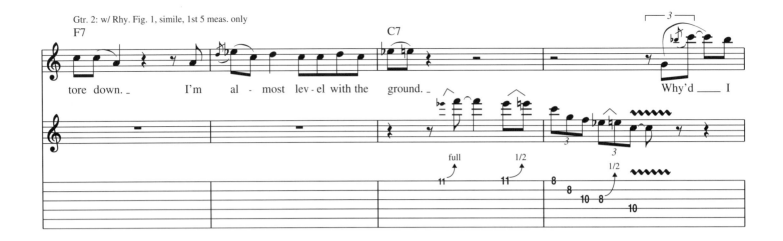

Gtr. 2: w/ Rhy. Fig. 1, simile, 1st 5 meas. only

tore down. _ I'm al - most lev - el with the ground. _ Why'd ____ I

feel _ like this _ when _ my ba - by can't be found? _

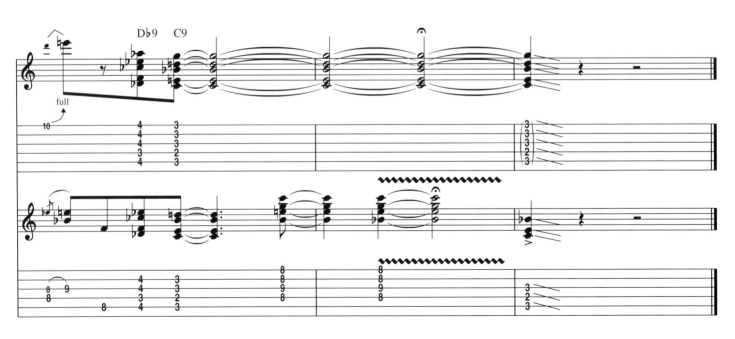

Ice Pick

By Albert Collins

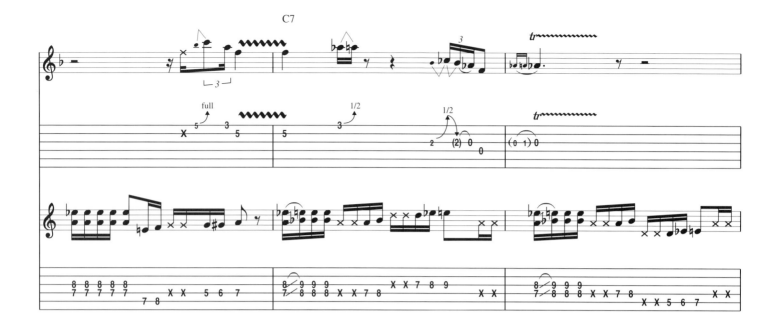

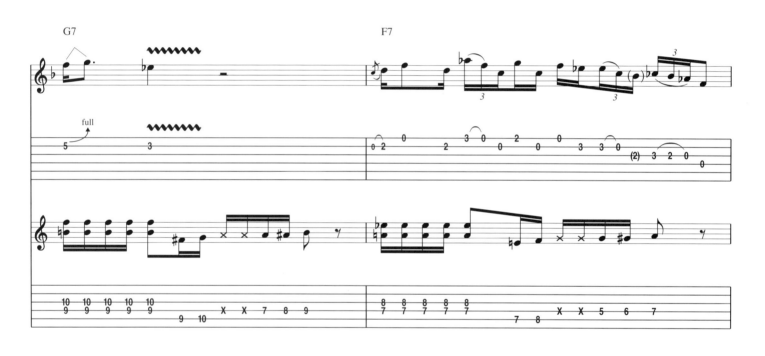

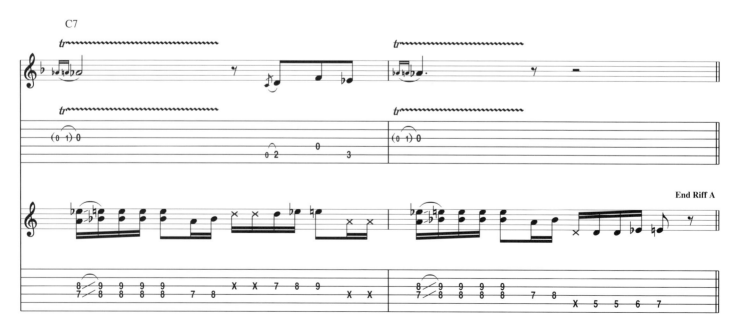

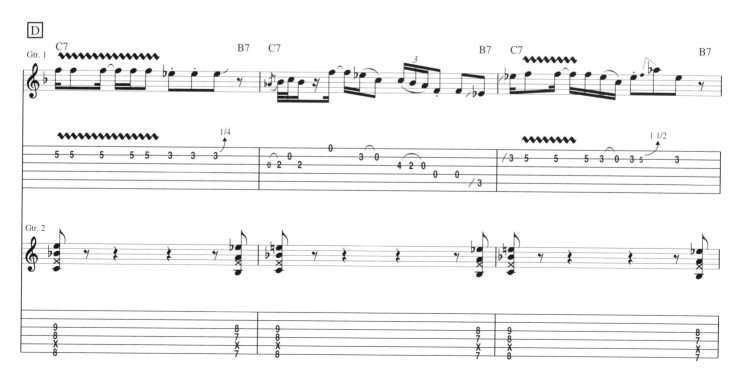

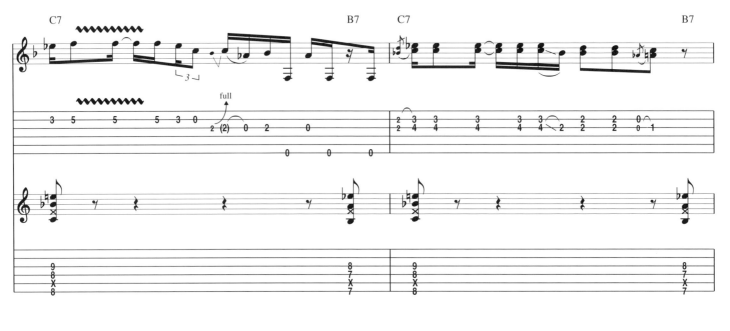

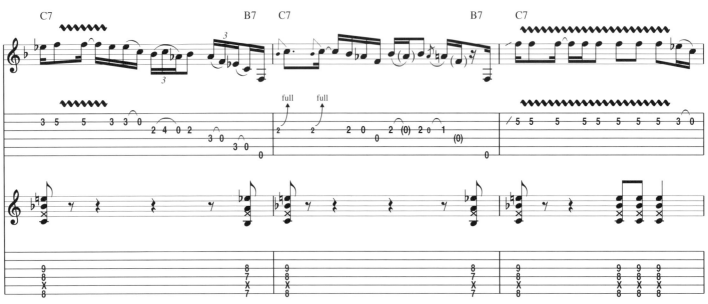

Gtr. 2: w/ Riff A, last 8 meas.

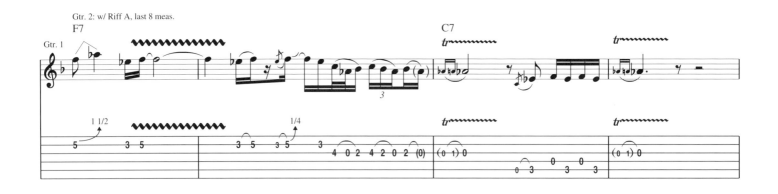

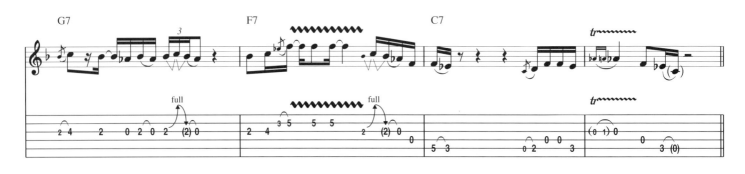

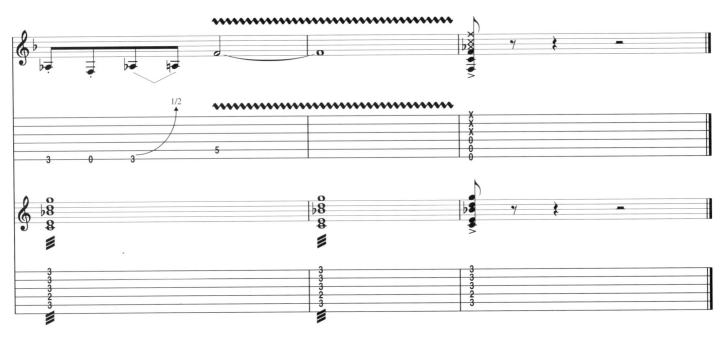

It Hurts Me Too

Words and Music by Mel London

Open D Tuning:
①= D ④= D
②= A ⑤= A
③= F# ⑥= D

Intro
Slow Blues ♩. = 59

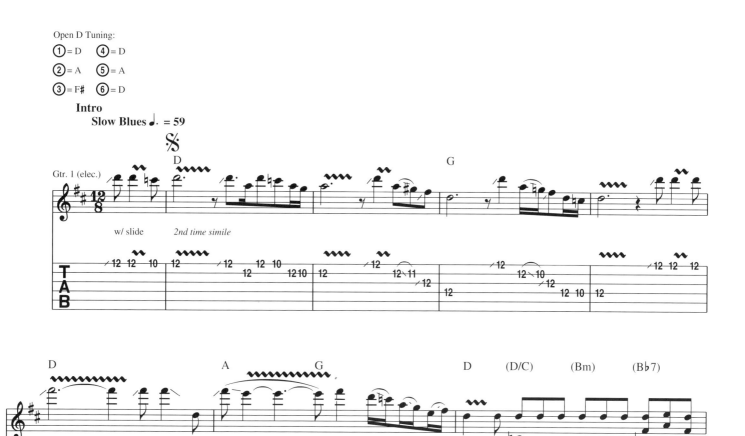

w/ slide   *2nd time simile*

1. You said   you was   hurt-ing, _____   you   al-most lost your
   _____ wom-an.   when you should love him
4. Now,   he   bet-ter   leave you,   Yes, ___ I   love
                                                 or   you bet-ter put him

Killing Floor

Words and Music by Chester Burnett

Gtr 2: Tune down 1 step:
(low to high) D–G–C–F–A–D

Intro

Moderately ♩ = 104

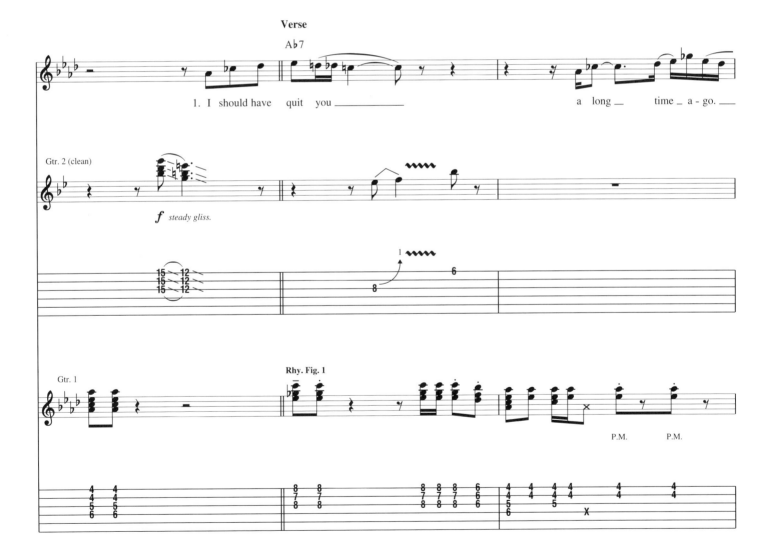

*Two gtrs. arr. for one.
**Chord symbols reflect basic harmony.

I should have quit you, ba - by,

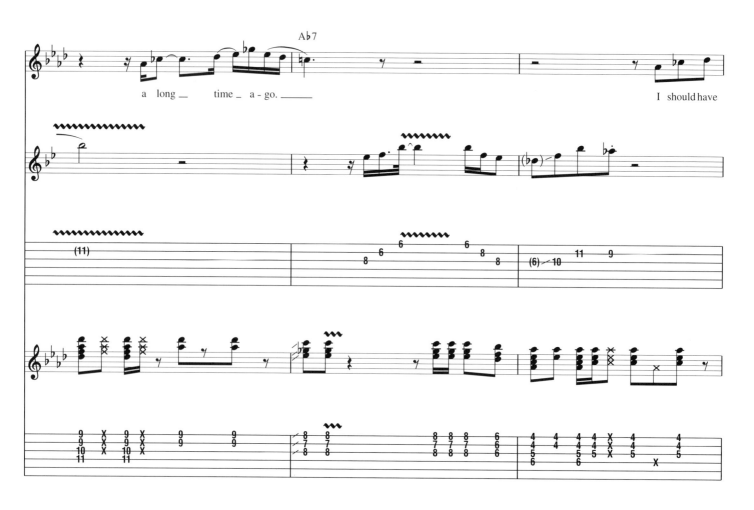

a long time a-go.

I should have

quit you, ba - by, ____ and went on ____ to Mex-i - co.

Verse
Gtr. 1: w/ Rhy. Fig. 1 (1st 8 meas.)

2. If I had a fol - lowed my first ___ mind, ___

End Rhy. Fig. 1

if I had a fol - lowed _____

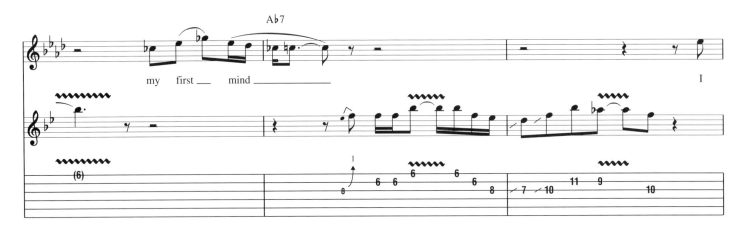

my first ___ mind _____

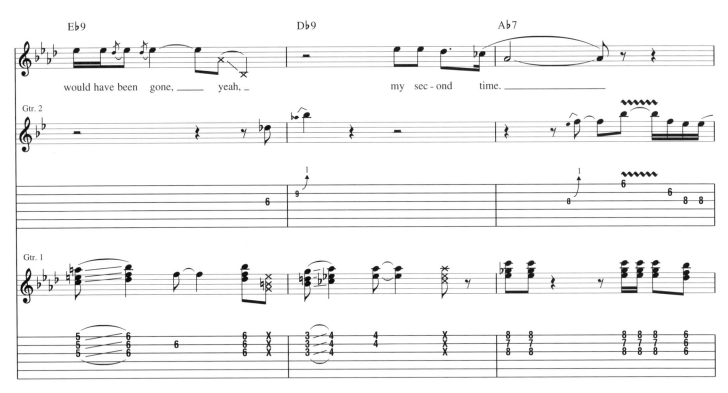

would have been gone, _____ yeah, _

my sec - ond time. _____

Gtr. 2

Gtr. 1

Guitar Solo

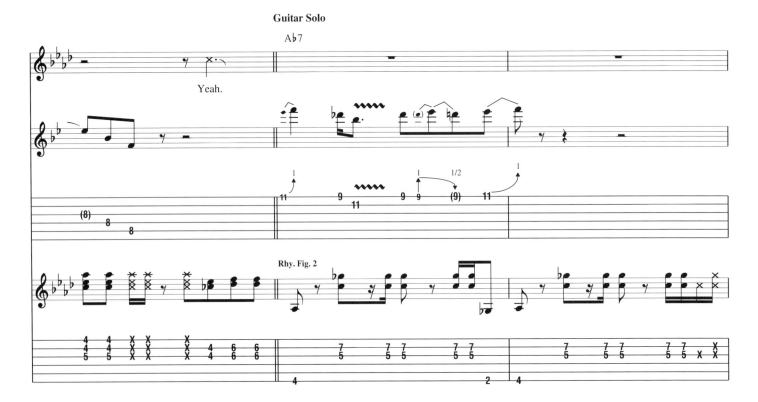

Yeah.

Rhy. Fig. 2

Verse

Gtr. 1: w/ Rhy. Fig. 1

3. I should have went on ___ when my friends come from Mex - i - co and

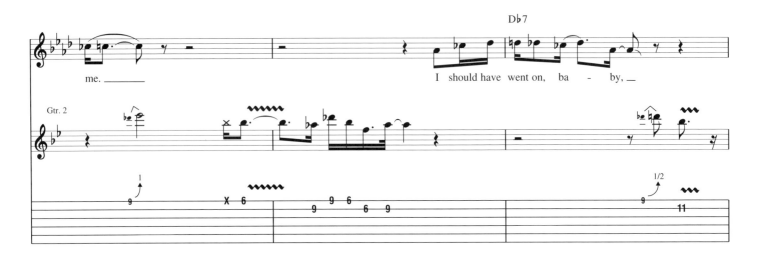

me. ___ I should have went on, ba - by, ___

when my friends ___ come from Mex - i - co ___ and me. ___ Now, ___ fool -

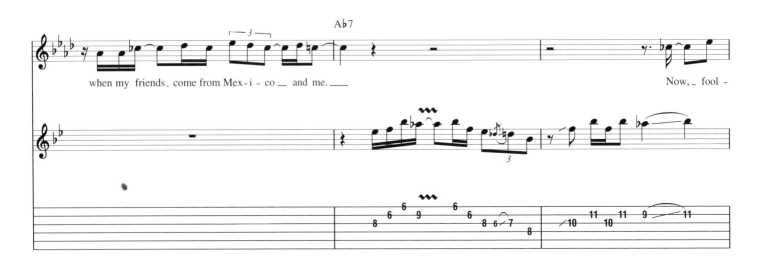

ing 'round with you, dar - ling, ___ you got me on the kill-ing floor. ___

Verse

Gtr. 1: w/ Rhy. Fig. 1

4. I know ___ I should have been gone. ___

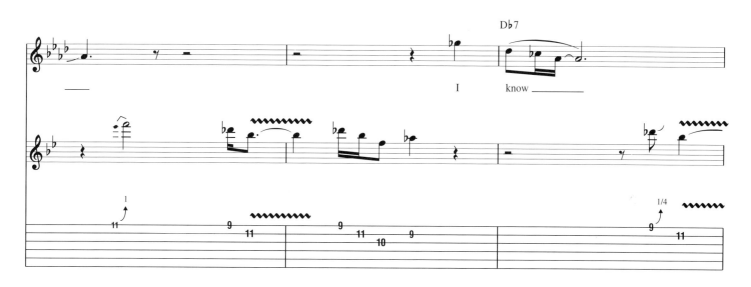

I know ___

I should have been gone. ___

Now

fool-ing 'round ___ with you, ba - by,

I let you put me on the kill-ing floor. ___

Guitar Solo

Gtr. 2: w/ Rhy. Fig. 1

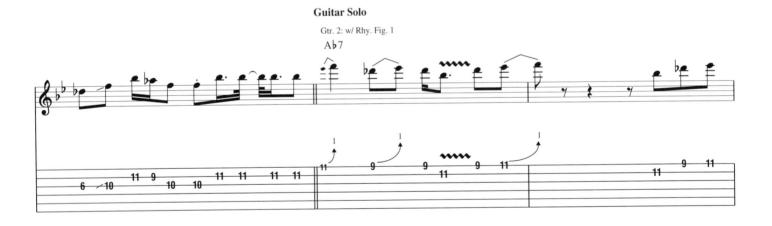

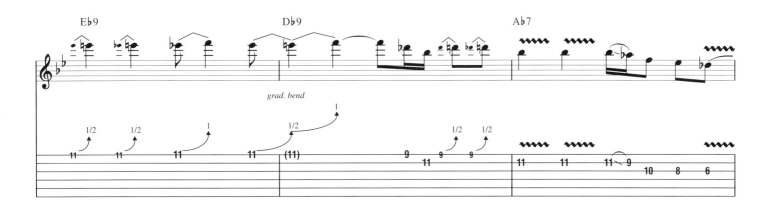

Begin fade

Gtr. 2: w/ Rhy. Fig. 2

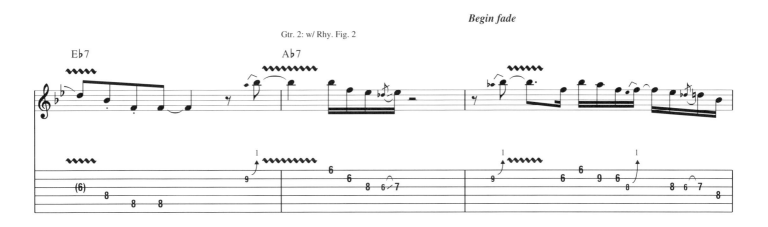

Fade out

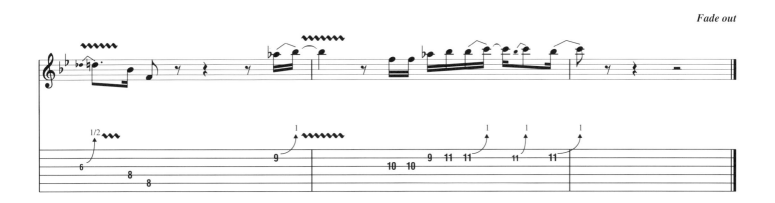

Kind Hearted Woman Blues

Words and Music by Robert Johnson

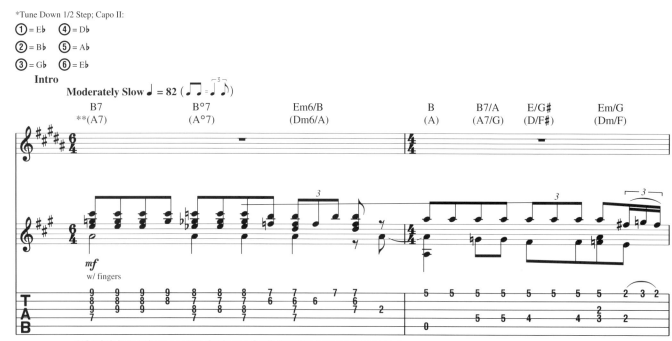

*Tune Down 1/2 Step; Capo II:

① = E♭   ④ = D♭
② = B♭   ⑤ = A♭
③ = G♭   ⑥ = E♭

**Symbols in parentheses represent chord names (implied tonality) respective to capoed guitar.
Symbols above reflect harmony implied by vocals. Capoed fret is "0" in TAB.

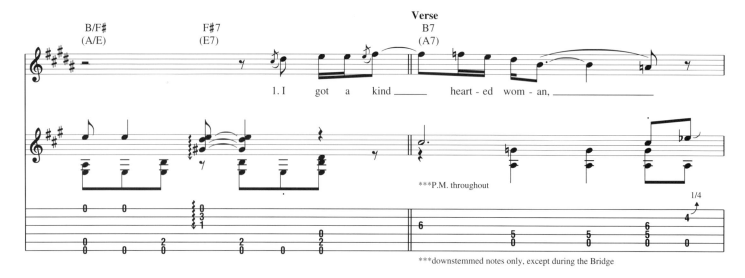

***downstemmed notes only, except during the Bridge

*Tunings were determined using the original 78s. To play along with the
Robert Johnson - The Complete Recordings CD set, Capo III.

* Resume P.M. on downstem notes.

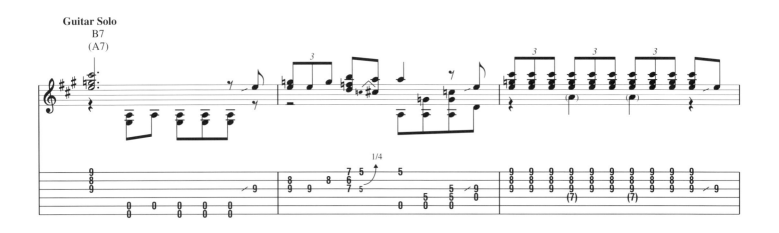

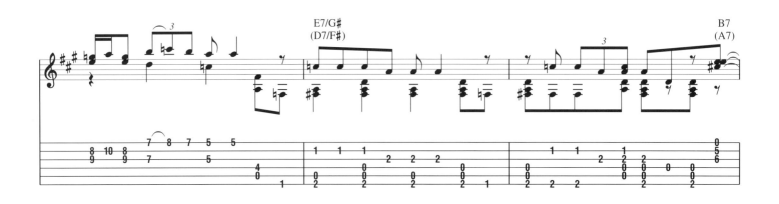

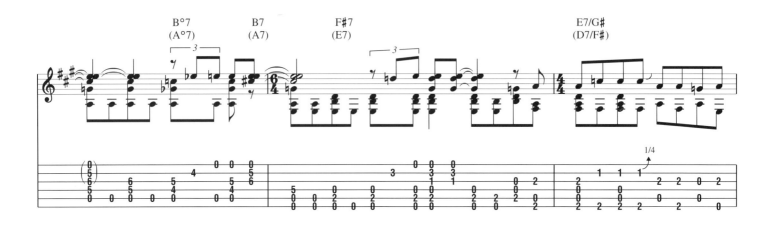

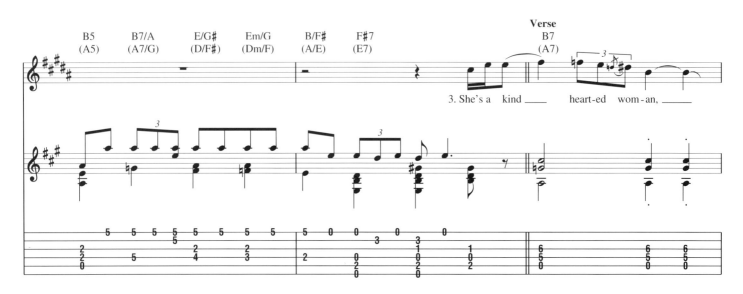

3. She's a kind ____ heart-ed wom-an, ____

Look on Yonder's Wall

By James Clark

Outro-Solo

Gtr. 1: w/ Rhy. Fig. 1, 1st 10 meas., simile

Mannish Boy

Written by McKinley Morgenfield (Muddy Waters), M.R. London and Ellas McDaniel

Gtr. 2 continues Fig. 2

Mary Ann

Words and Music by Ray Charles

Intro

Moderate Calypso ♩ = 112

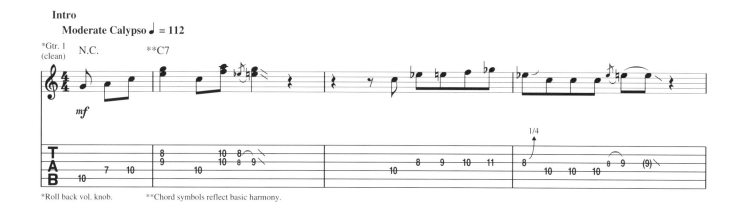

*Roll back vol. knob.   **Chord symbols reflect basic harmony.

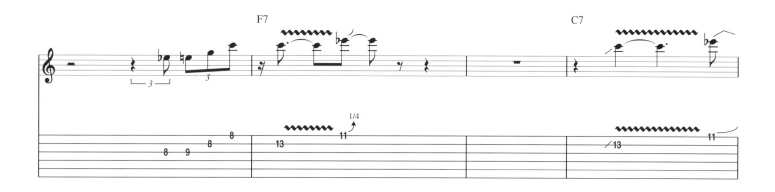

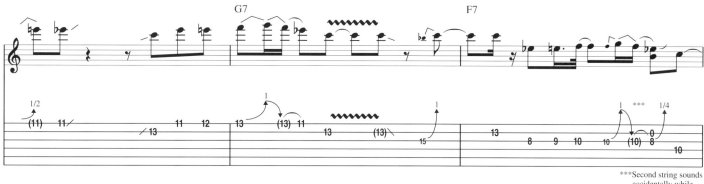

***Second string sounds
accidentally while
executing pulloff.

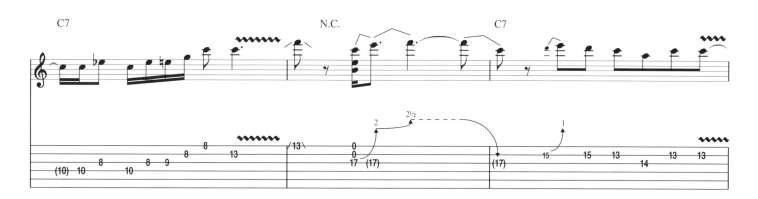

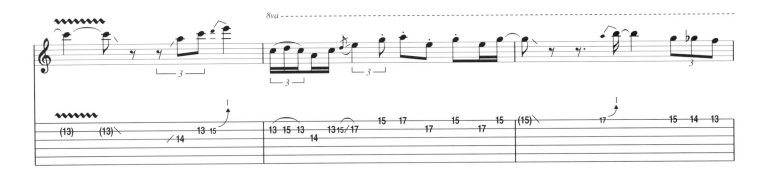

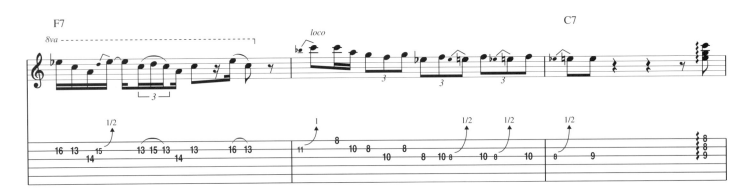

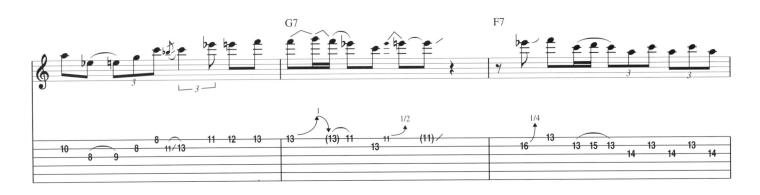

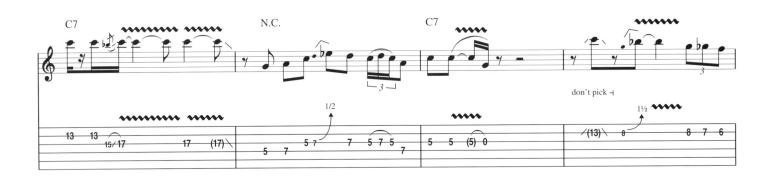

*Second A in triplet played with
third finger of left hand.

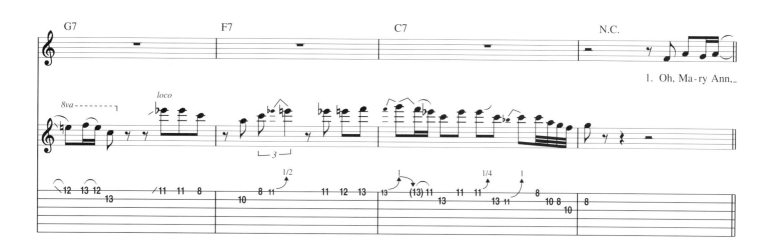

Verse

give you all _____ my lov-ing and _____ an-y-thing you want me to do. _____ 2. Oh, _____ Ma - ry

Verse

Ann, _____ I want you _____ by my side. _____

Ma-ry Ann, _____ Lord, _____ I want you by my side.

If _____ you love me, my love I will nev-er hide. _____

rake - - -

Guitar Solo

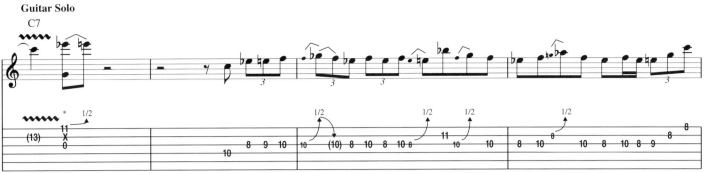

*Third string sounds accidentally while lifting third finger.

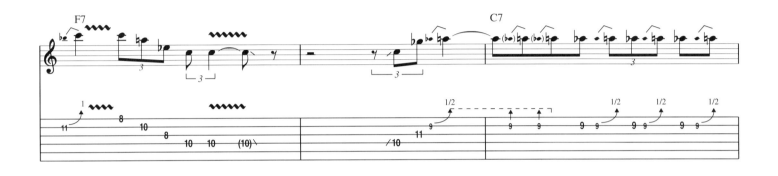

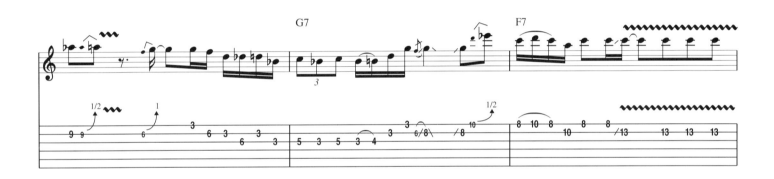

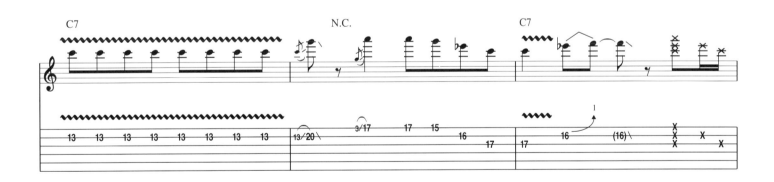

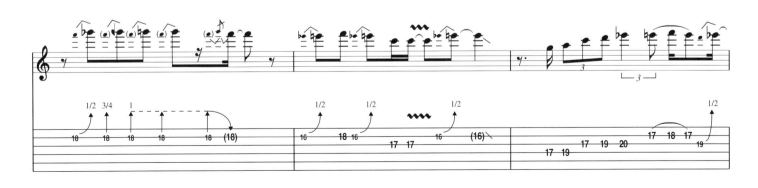

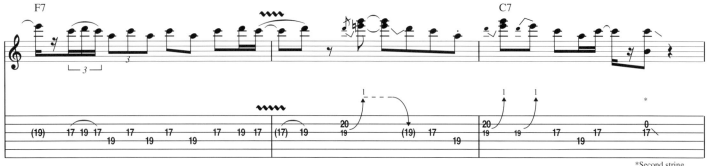

*Second string sounds accidentally while lifting index finger.

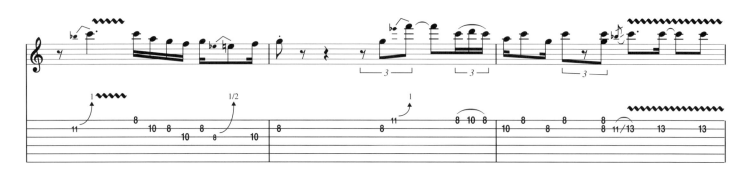

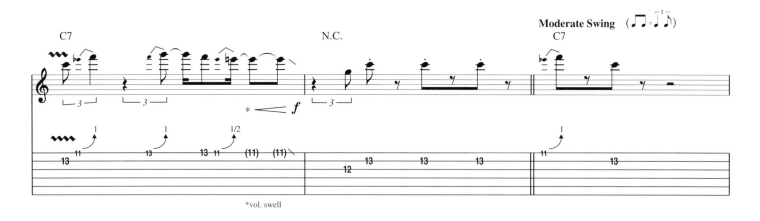

*vol. swell

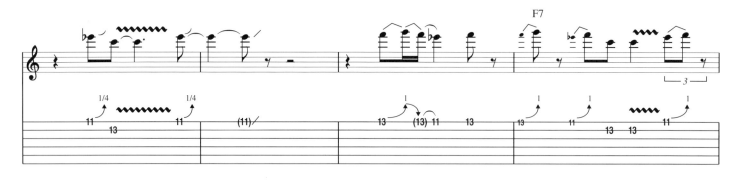

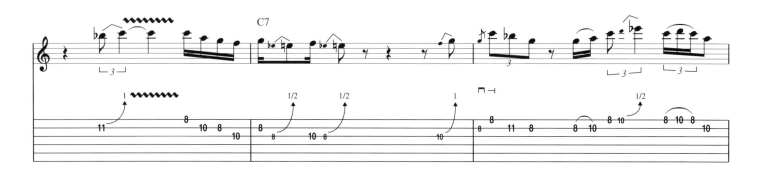

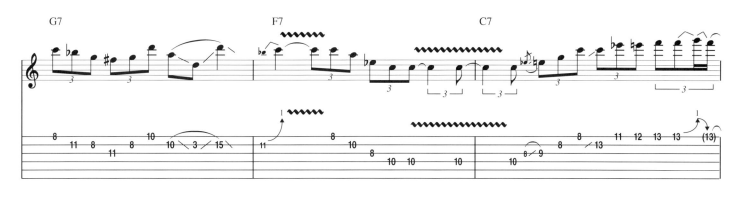

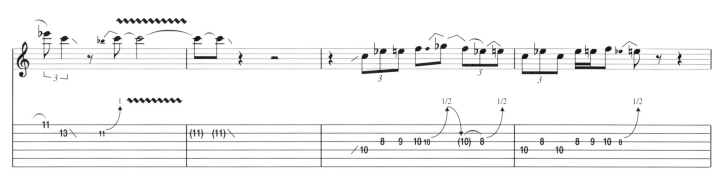

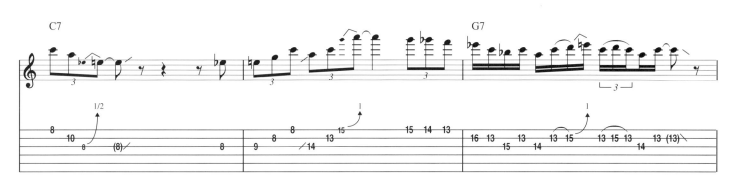

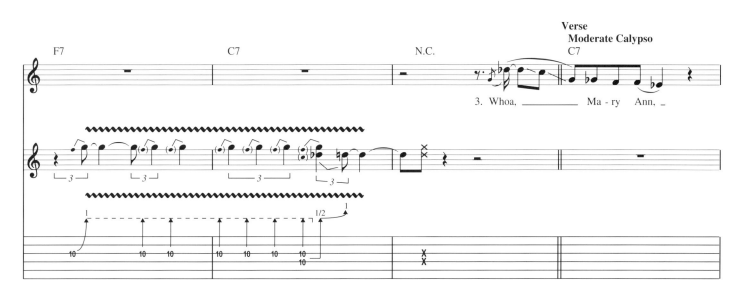

3. Whoa, _____ Ma - ry Ann, _

123

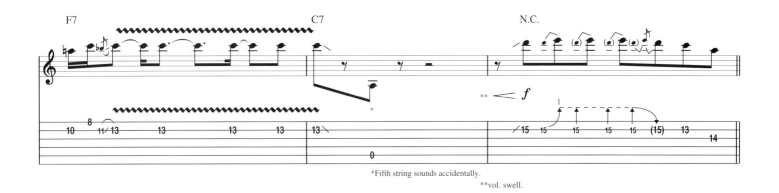

*Fifth string sounds accidentally.

**vol. swell.

Moderate Rock

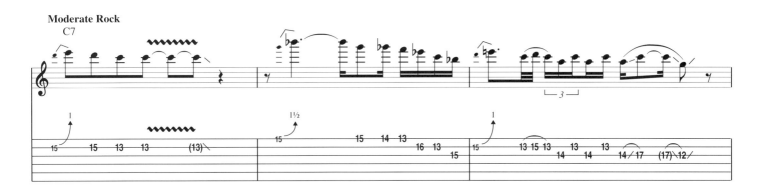

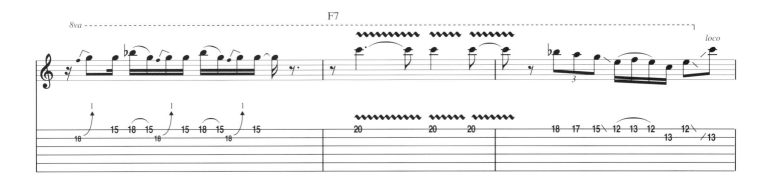

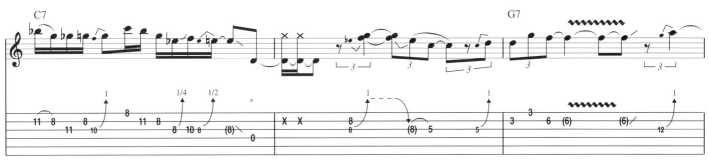

*Fourth string sounds accidentally.

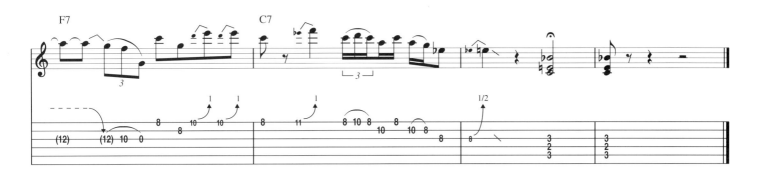

On My Knees

By Son Seals

2., 4. I sit and

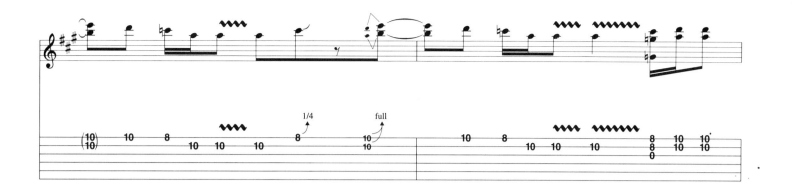

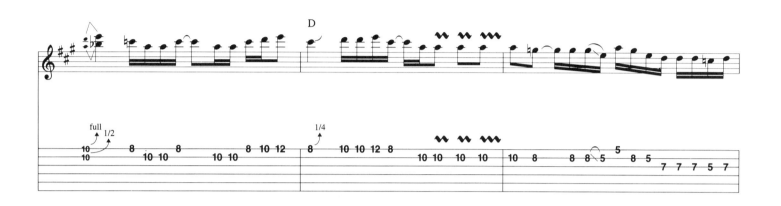

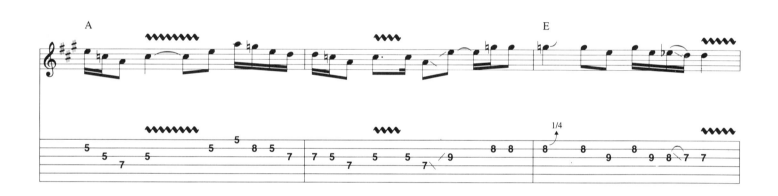

D.S. al Coda

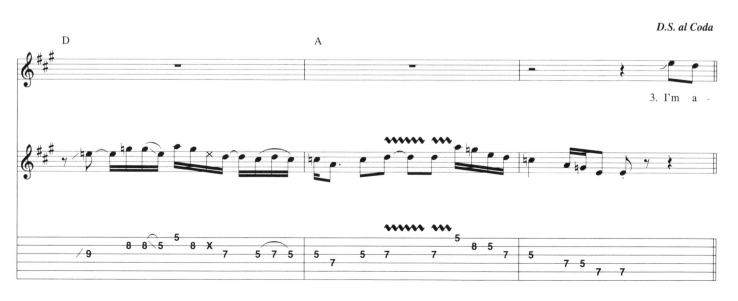

3. I'm a -

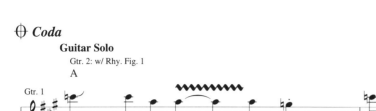

Coda

Guitar Solo

Gtr. 2: w/ Rhy. Fig. 1

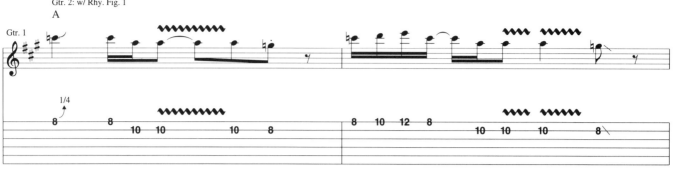

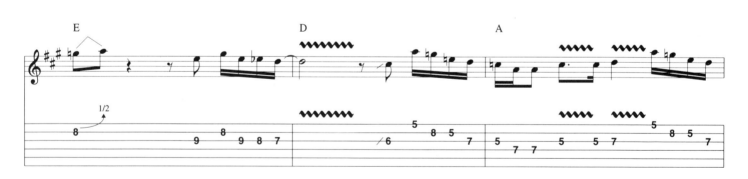

Piano Solo

Gtr. 1 tacet

Gtr. 2: w/ Rhy. Fig. 1, simile, till fade

Fade Out

130

Pride and Joy

Written by Stevie Ray Vaughan

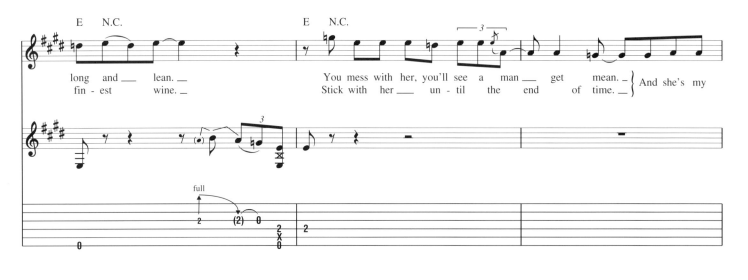

long and ___ lean.
fin - est wine. ___

You mess with her, you'll see a man ___ get mean. ___ } And she's my
Stick with her ___ un - til the end of time. ___

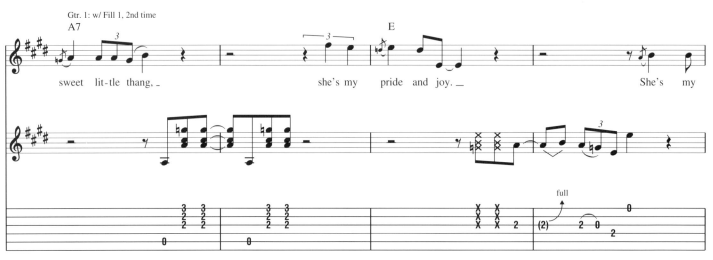

Gtr. 1: w/ Fill 1, 2nd time

sweet lit - tle thang, ___   she's my pride and joy. ___   She's my

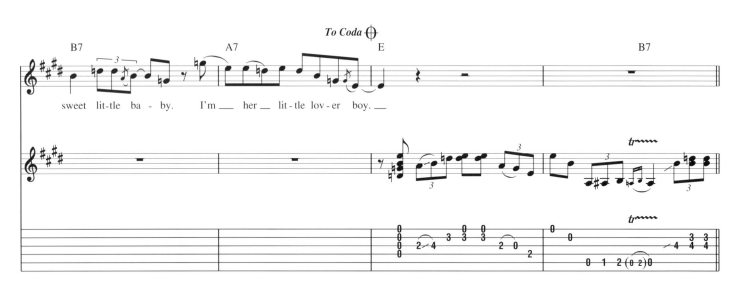

To Coda ⊕

sweet lit - tle ba - by.   I'm ___ her ___ lit - tle lov - er boy. ___

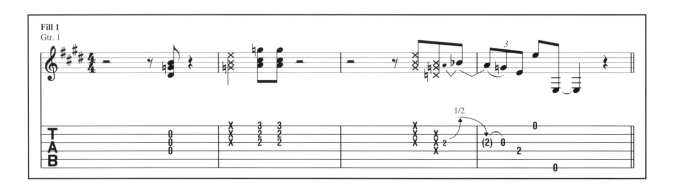

Fill 1
Gtr. 1

Guitar Solo

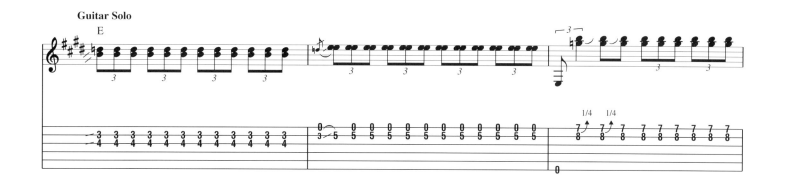

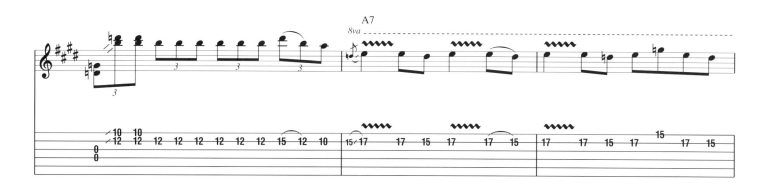

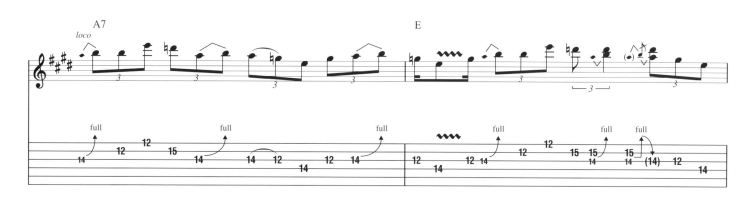

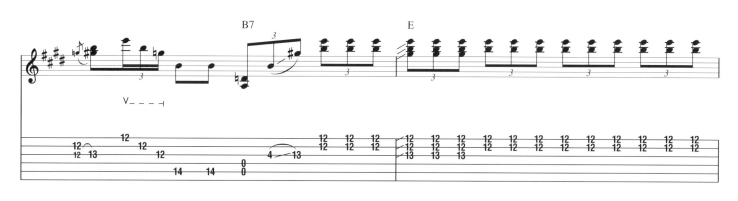

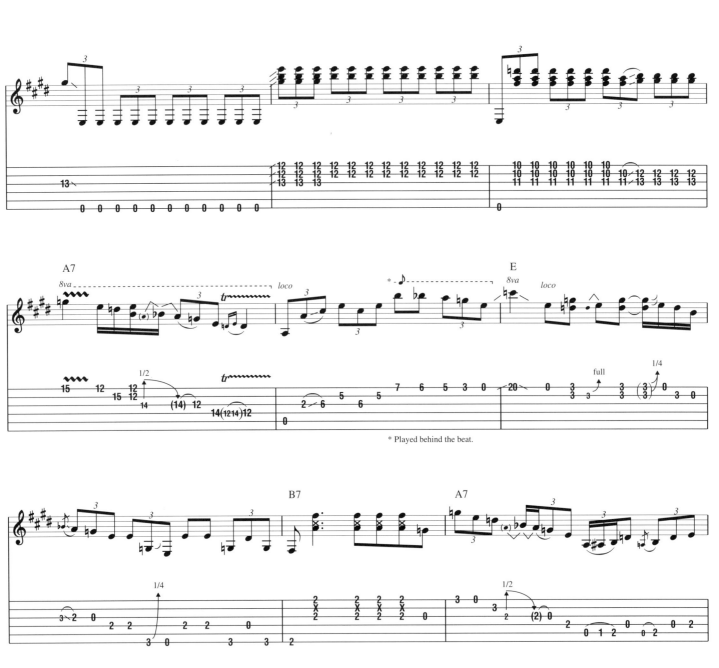

* Played behind the beat.

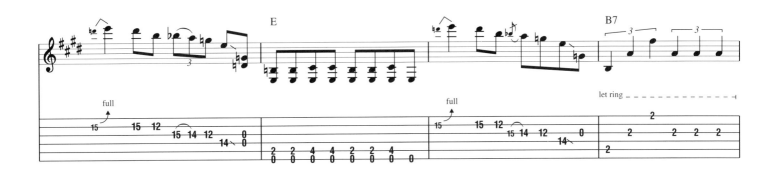

D.S. al Coda

4. Yeah, I

Coda

5. Yeah, I

Verse

love my ba-by, my heart and soul. Love like ours ah, won't

nev-er, nev-er, nev-er grow old. ___ She's my pride and joy. ___

She's my sweet lit-tle ba - by, I'm ___ her ___ lit - tle lov - er boy. ___

Outro-Guitar Solo

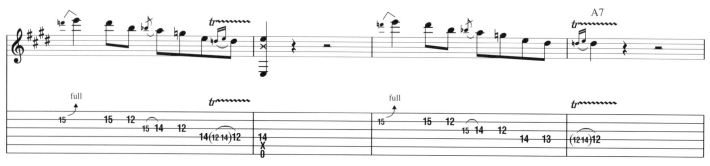

* Played as even eighth notes.

Reconsider Baby

Words and Music by Lowell Fulson

oh, how I hate __ to see you go. __   And the way_

__ that I will miss you, __   I guess you will nev - er know. __   2. We've been to-geth -

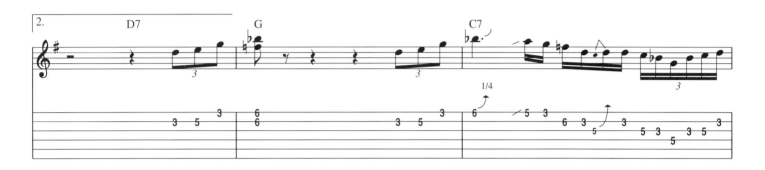

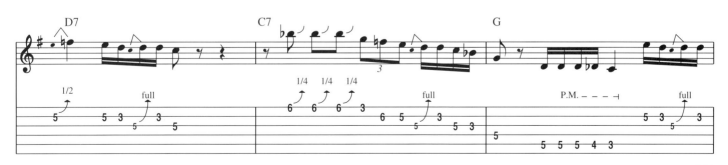

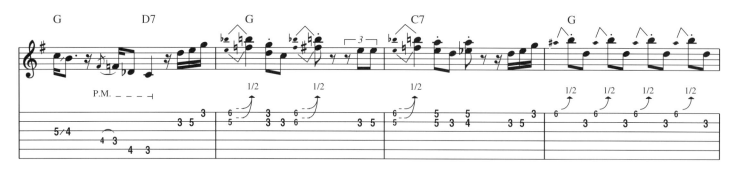

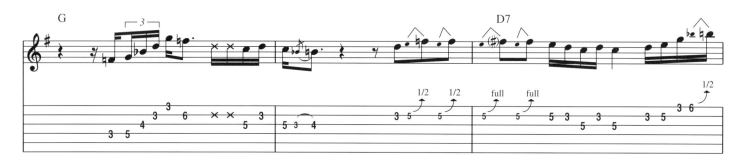

D.S. (3rd verse) al Coda

3. You said you once

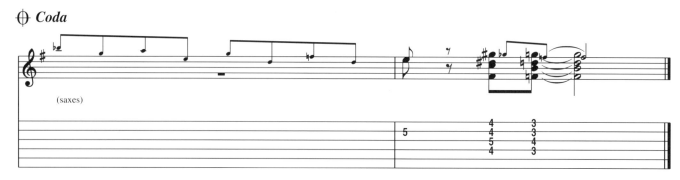

(saxes)

Additional Verses:

2. We've been together so long to have to separate this way.
   We've been together so long to have to separate this way.
   I'm gonna let you go ahead on, baby, pray that you'll come back home some day.

3. You said you once had loved me, but now I guess you have changed your mind.
   You said you once had loved me, but now I guess you have changed your mind.
   Why don't you reconsider, baby, give yourself just a little more time.

Red House

Jimi Hendrix

Tune Down 1/2 Step:

① = Eb ④ = Db

② = Bb ⑤ = Ab

③ = Gb ⑥ = Eb

Intro **Moderately Slow Blues** ♩. = 64

* Transcriptions written as if gtr. were tuned normally.

† Gtr. 2 (Noel Redding)

* Notes in parentheses are sounded unintentionally w/tip of 3rd finger, as a result of the A to B bend on the B string.

† On neck pickup w/treble off, simulating the sound of a bass.

*slightly "behind the beat"

I got a bad, bad _ feel - in', uh, that my ba - by _ don't live here no

more. *Spoken: She did-n't tell me noth-in' a - bout it eith - er.* That's al-right, I

still got my gui-tar. _ *Look out, ba-by!* Yeah! _____

Guitar Solo

ba - by don't love me no more, _____   oh, I know her sis - ter will.

Yeah.   *Spoken: How was that?*

Riding With the King

Words and Music by John Hiatt

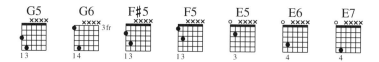

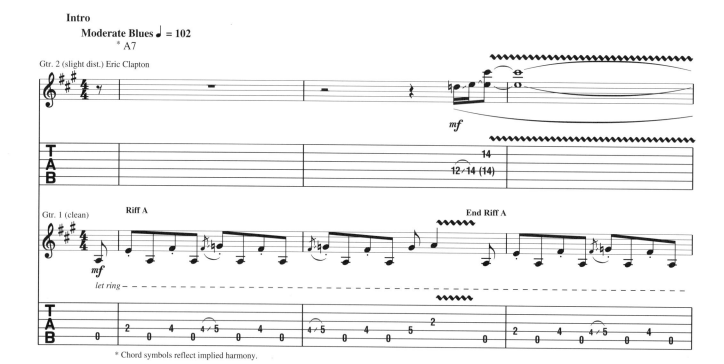

* Chord symbols reflect implied harmony.

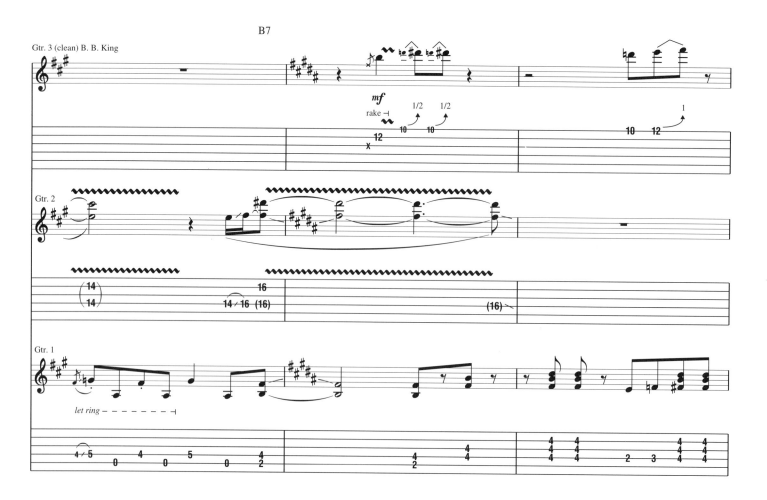

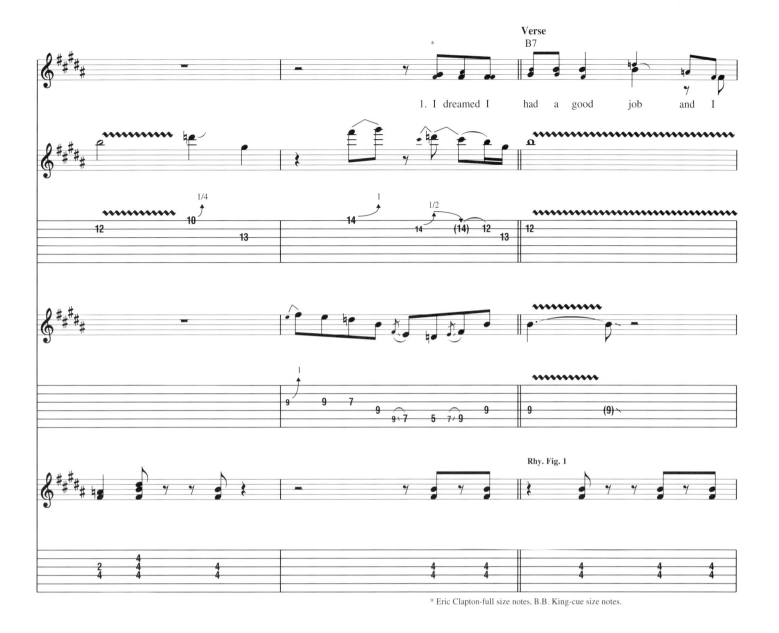

* Eric Clapton-full size notes, B.B. King-cue size notes.

Our hard earned dol - lars on a cup - id doll. __

No pret - ty chick is gon - na make __ me crawl.

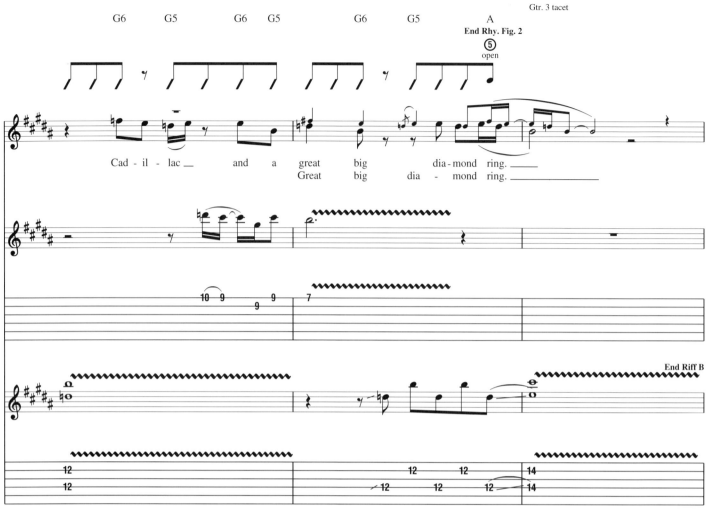

* Cue notes are female harmony (next 2 meas.).
  Eric Clapton upstem notes,
  B.B. King downstem notes.

**Eric Clapton-full size notes,
B.B. King-cue size notes,

158

Bridge

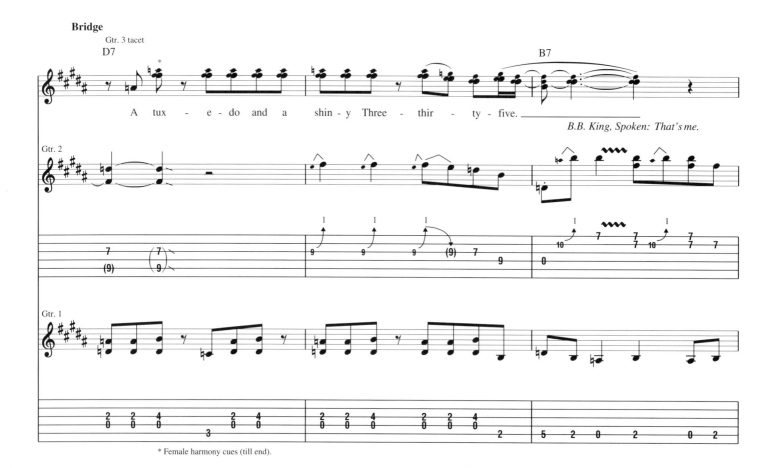

A tux - e - do and a shin - y Three - thir - ty - five. _____

B.B. King, Spoken: That's me.

* Female harmony cues (till end).

You can see it in his face, the blues is his life. __

Ha, ha, ha.

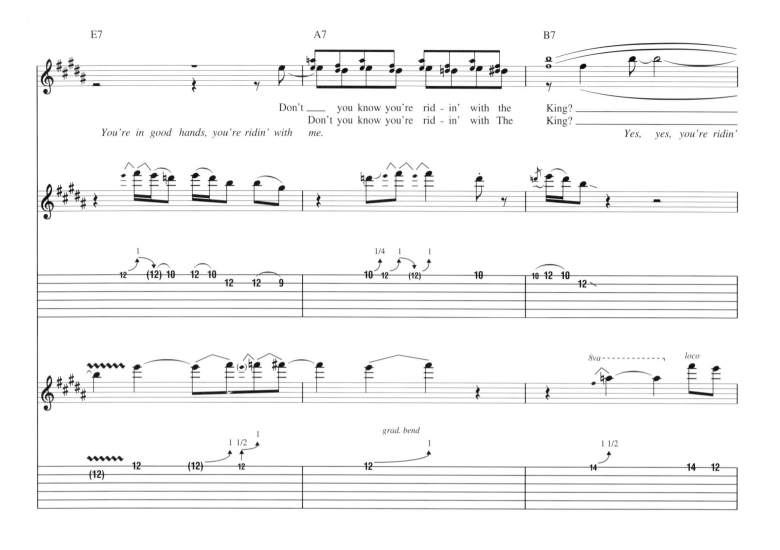

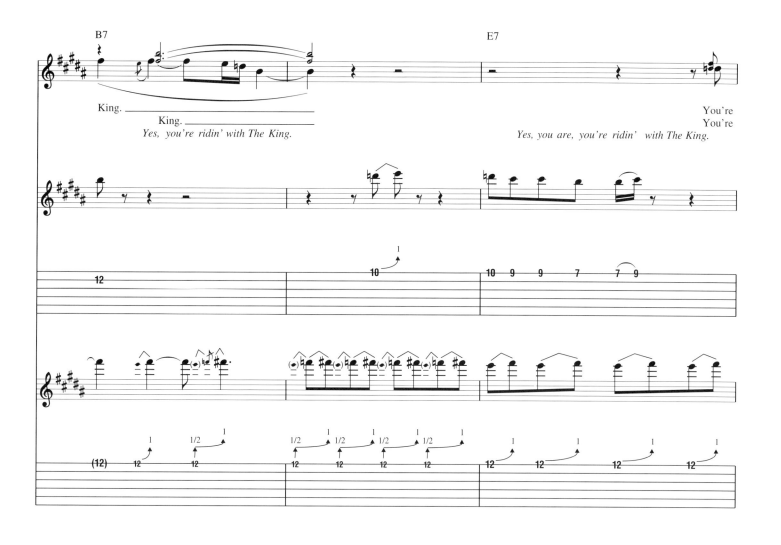

King. _____ King. _____
Yes, you're ridin' with The King.

You're
You're
Yes, you are, you're ridin' with The King.

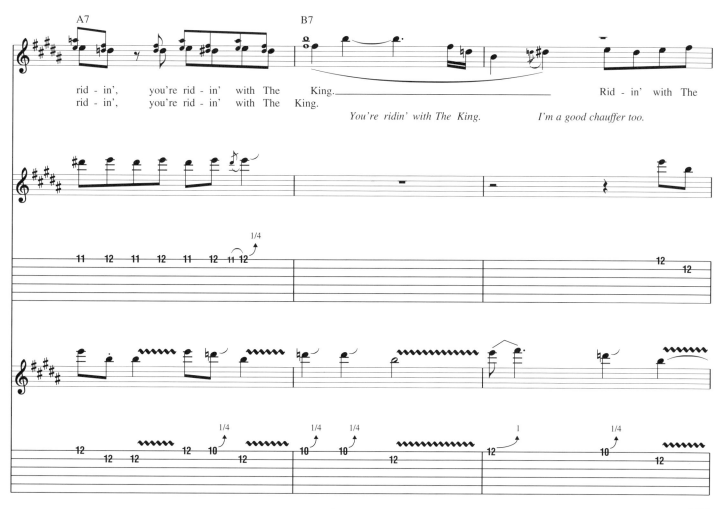

rid - in', you're rid - in' with The
rid - in', you're rid - in' with The

King. _____
King.
You're ridin' with The King.

Rid - in' with The

I'm a good chauffer too.

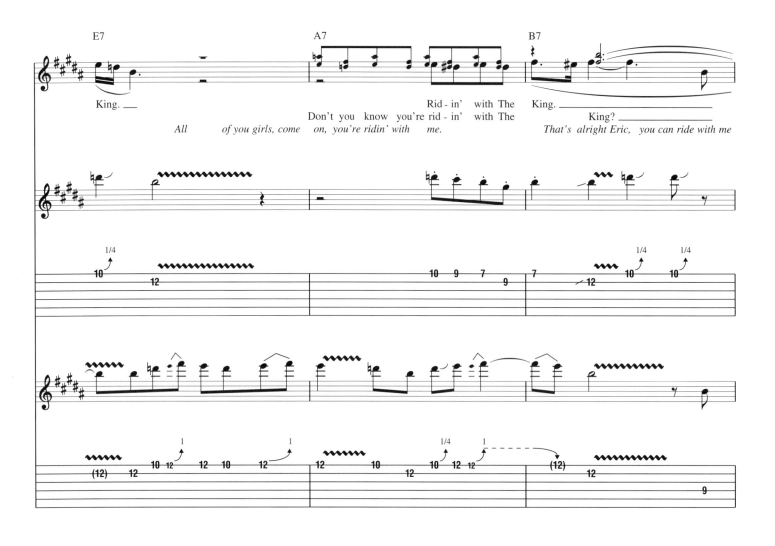

King. _____

King. _____

Rid - in' with The King.

Don't you know you're rid - in' with The King? _____

All of you girls, come on, you're ridin' with me.

That's alright Eric, you can ride with me

Begin fade

_____ Rid - in' with The King. _____

You're rid - in', you're rid - in, you're rid - in' with The Rid - in' with The

too if you feel like it.

Yes, you're ridin' with The King.

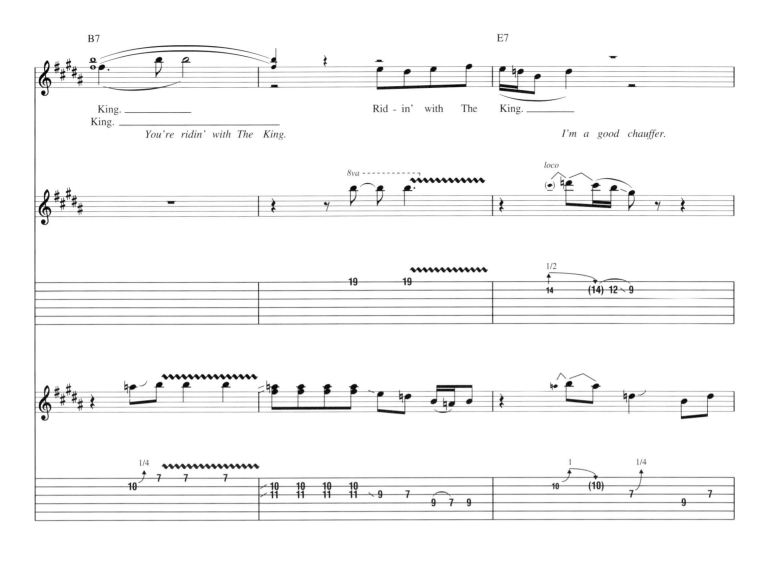

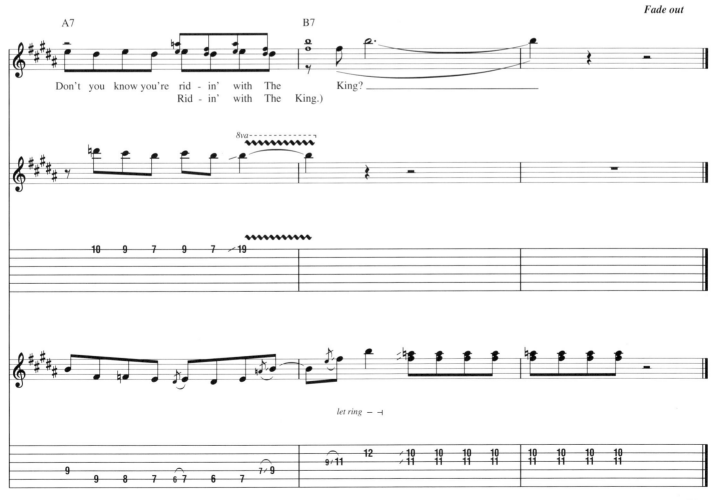

Rollin' And Tumblin'

Written by McKinley Morgenfield (Muddy Waters)

* Symbols in parentheses represent chord names respective to capoed guitar. Symbols above reflect actual sounding chord.

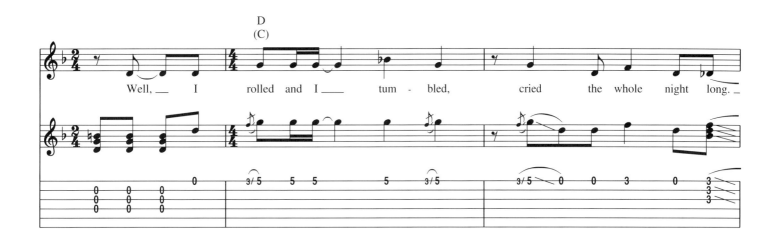

Well, __ I rolled and I __ tum - bled, cried the whole night long. __

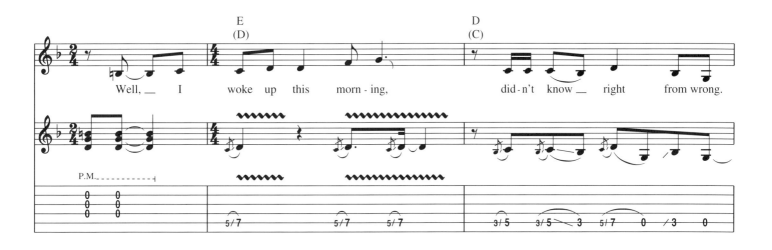

Well, __ I woke up this morn - ing, did - n't know __ right from wrong.

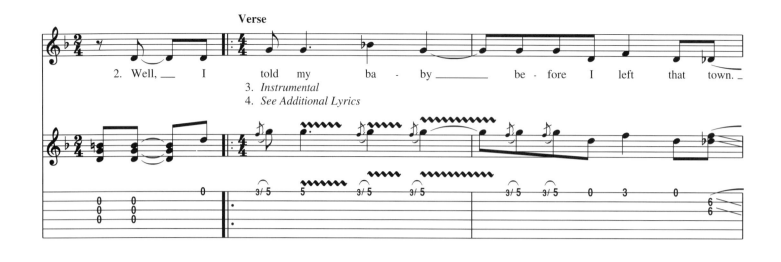

Verse

2. Well, ___ I   told   my   ba - by _____   be - fore   I   left   that   town. ___
3. *Instrumental*
4. *See Additional Lyrics*

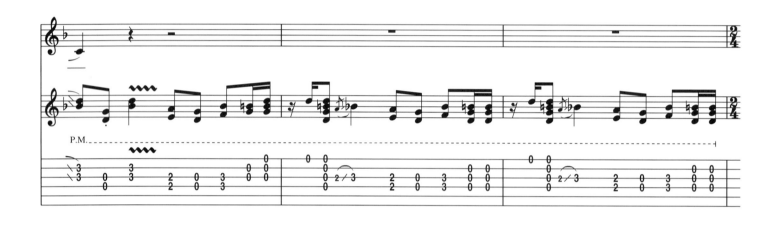

P.M.⌐ ───┐

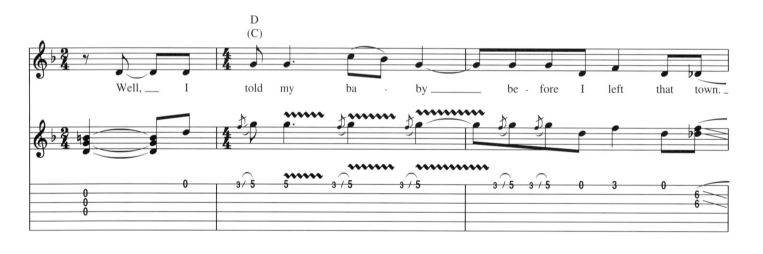

D
(C)

Well, ___ I   told   my   ba - by _____   be - fore   I   left   that   town. ___

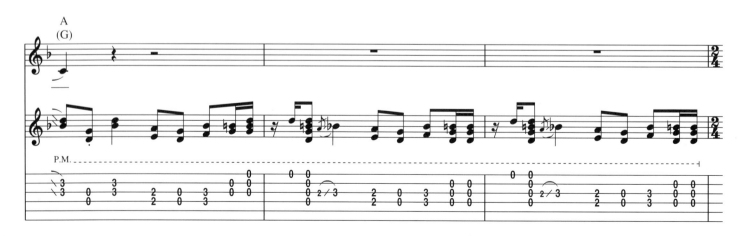

A
(G)

P.M.⌐ ───┐

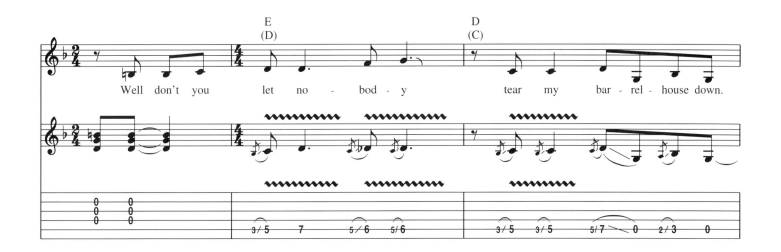

Well don't you let no - bod - y tear my bar - rel - house down.

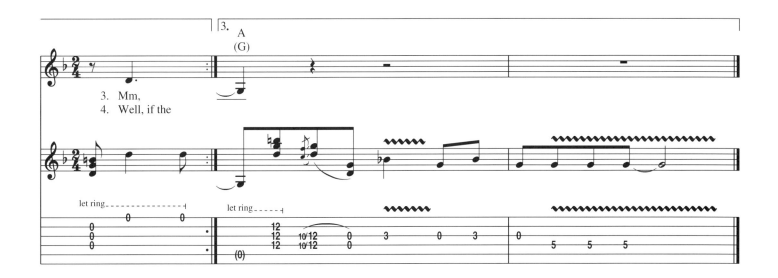

3. Mm,
4. Well, if the

Additional Lyrics

4. Well, if the river was whiskey and I was a diving duck,
   Well, if the river was whiskey and I was a diving duck,
   Well, I would dive to the bottom and never would I come up.

5. Well, I could have had religion this bad old someday.
   Well, I could have had religion this bad old someday.
   Well now, whiskey and women would not let me get away.

The Sky Is Crying

Words and Music by Elmore James

Tune down 1/2 step

Slow Blues ($\sharp. = 55$)

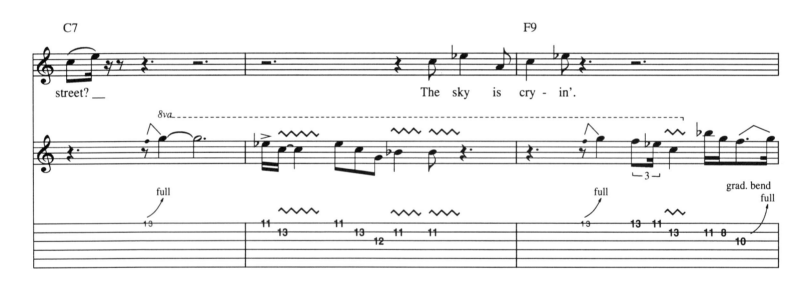

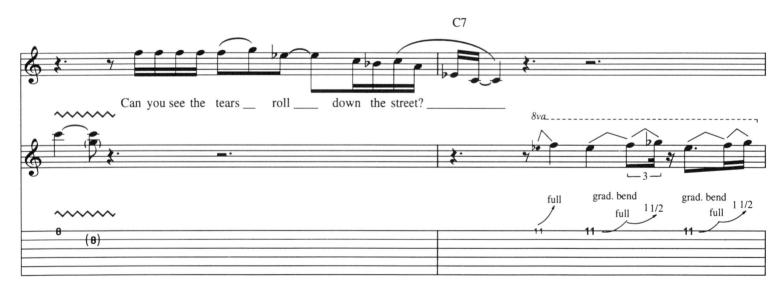

that my ba - by don't _____ love me no more.

You know the sky, the sky's been cry - in', yeah!

Can you see the tears _____ roll - in' down my nose?

Statesboro Blues

Words and Music by Will McTell

Gtr. 2: Standard Tuning
Gtr. 1: Open E Tuning:
①=E ④=E
②=B ⑤=B
③=G# ⑥=E

Intro
Moderate Shuffle ♩ = 125

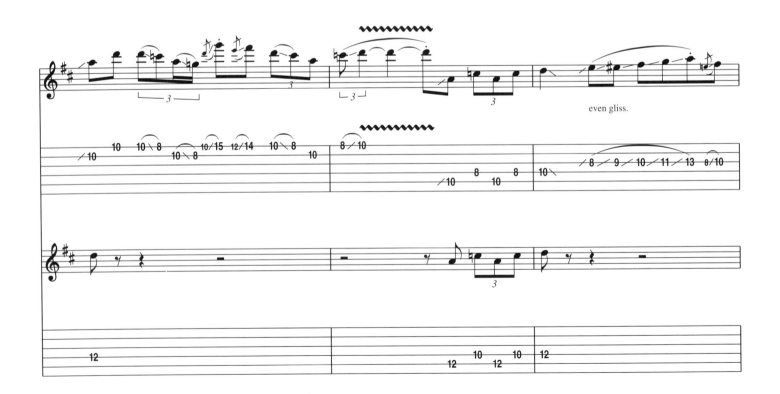

even gliss.

* D7

G7

D7

even gliss.

Rhy. Fig. 1

semi-P.M. throughout

* Chord symbols outline general harmony throughout.

* Slide positioned halfway
between 13th and 14th fret.

G7

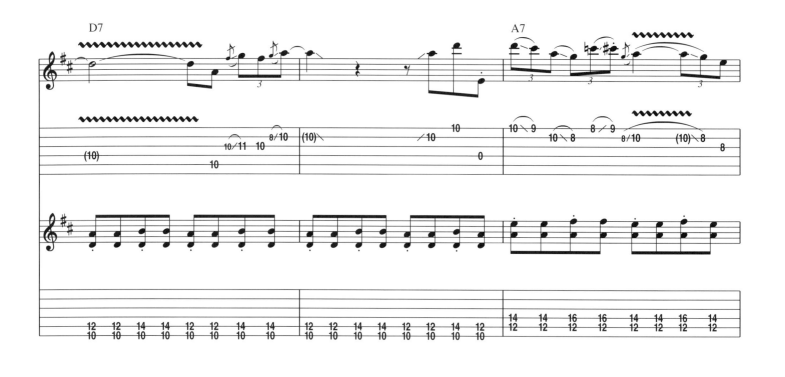

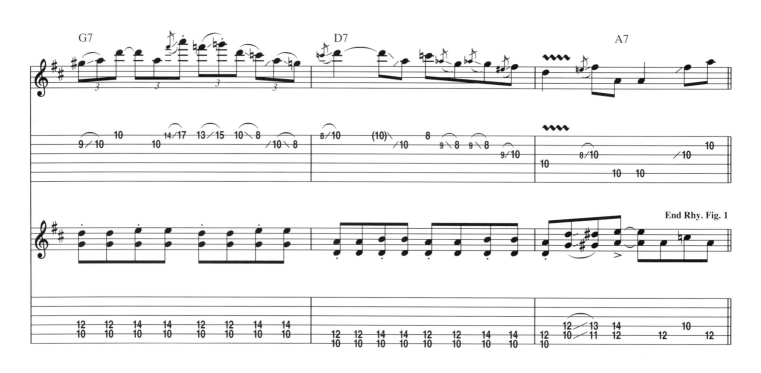

Verse

Gtr. 2: w/ Rhy. Fig. 1, simile

1. Wake up, ma - ma, turn your lamp down __ low. __

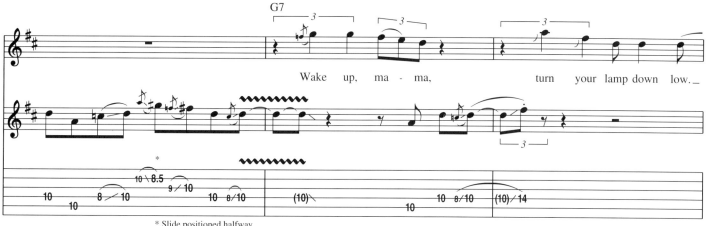

Wake up, ma-ma, turn your lamp down low. ___

* Slide positioned halfway
between 8th and 9th fret.

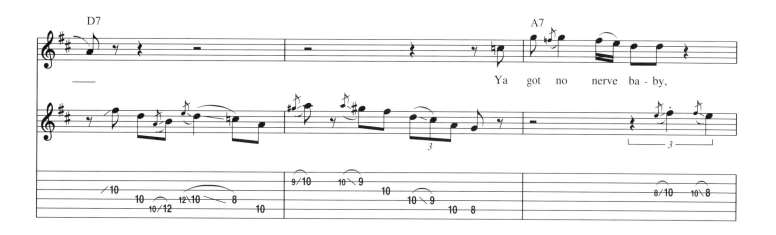

___ Ya got no nerve ba-by,

ya turn Un-cle John from your door. ___

Verse

Gtr. 2: w/ Rhy. Fig. 1

2. I woke___ up this morn - in' an' I had them States-bo-ro blues. ___

* Slide positioned halfway
between 8th & 9th fret

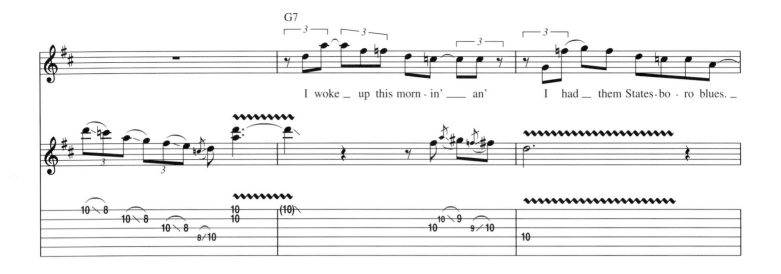

I woke __ up this morn - in' ___ an' __ I had __ them States - bo - ro blues. __

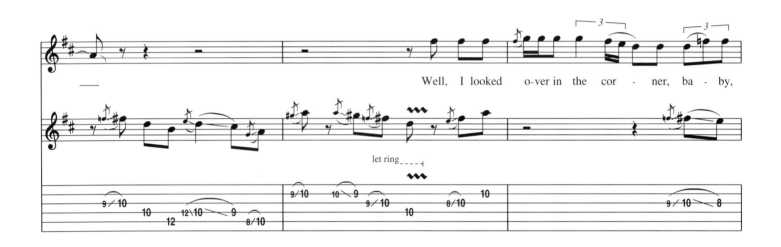

___ Well, I looked __ o-ver in the cor - ner, ba - by,

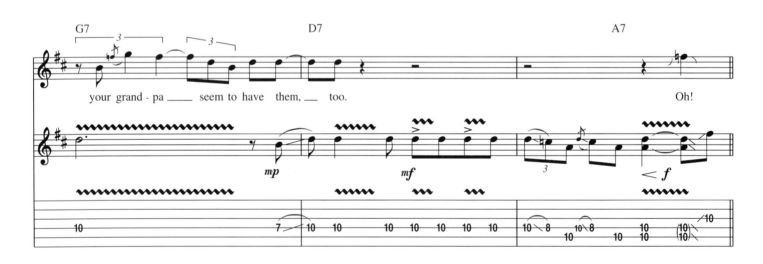

your grand - pa ___ seem to have them, __ too. Oh!

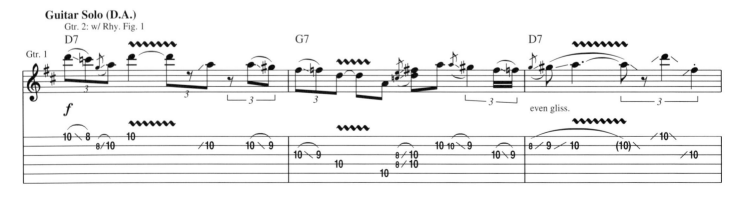

Guitar Solo (D.A.)
Gtr. 2: w/ Rhy. Fig. 1

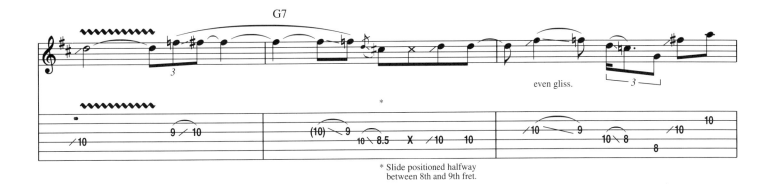

G7

* Slide positioned halfway
between 8th and 9th fret.

D7

A7

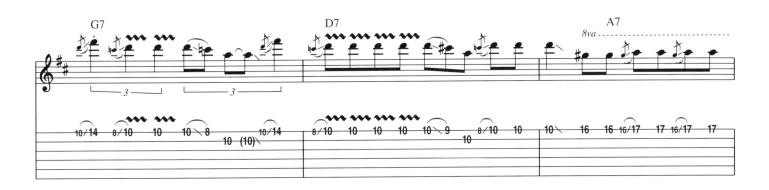

G7

D7

A7

Gtr. 2: w/ Rhy. Fig. 1, 1st 10 meas., simile

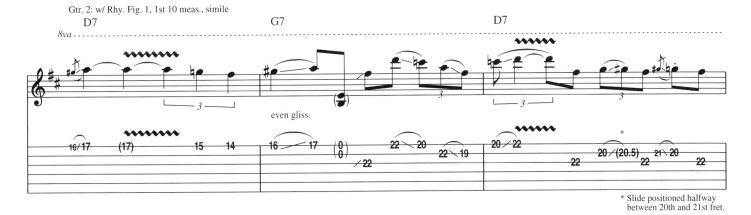

D7

G7

D7

even gliss.

* Slide positioned halfway
between 20th and 21st fret.

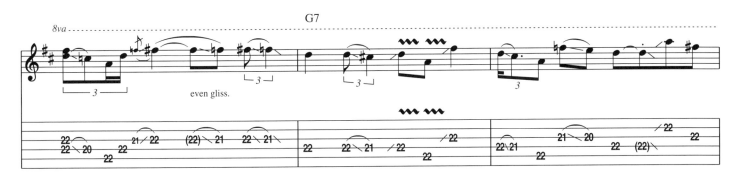

G7

even gliss.

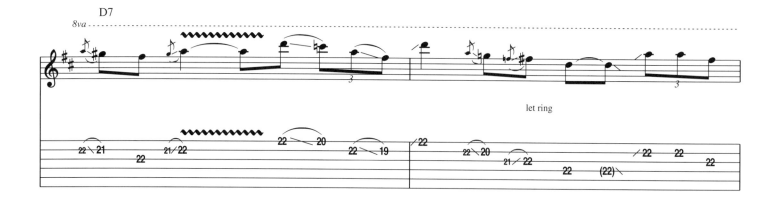

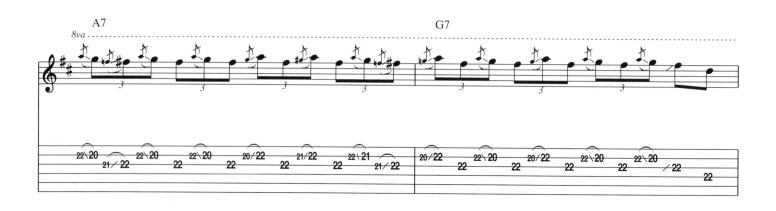

3. Well, my ma-ma died and left me, my

pa - pa died and left me.   I ain't good look-in', ba - by   want some-one sweet and ____ kind. ____

I'm go-in' to the coun-try,   ba - by, do you wan - na go? ____

If   you   can't   make it, ba - by,

* Slide positioned halfway between 8th and 9th fret.

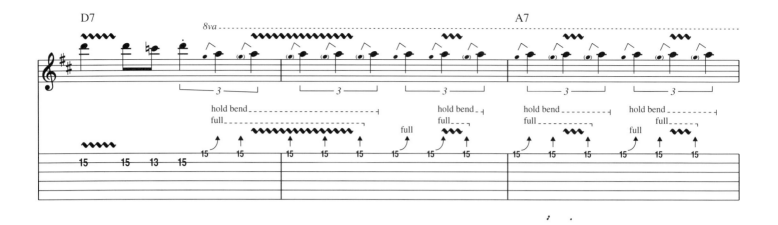

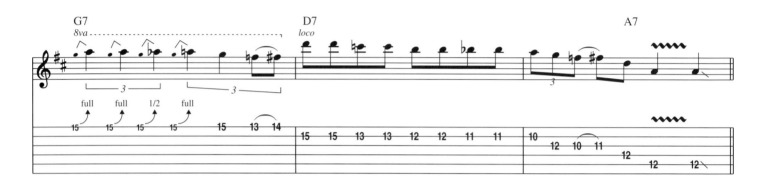

Verse

Gtr. 2: w/ Rhy. Fig. 1

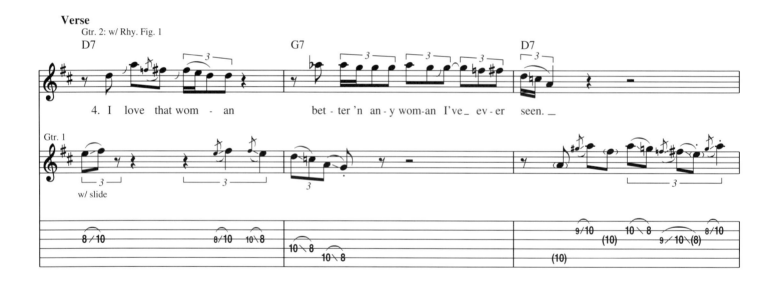

4. I love that wom - an bet - ter 'n an - y wom-an I've_ ev - er seen._

Well I _____ love that wom - an, bet - ter 'n an - y wom-an I've _ ev - er

* Slide positioned halfway between 8th & 9th fret.

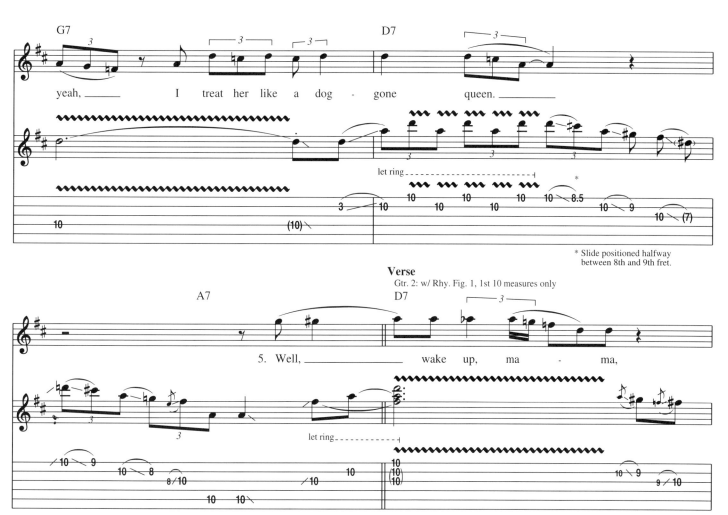

* Slide positioned halfway between 8th and 9th fret.

Verse
Gtr. 2: w/ Rhy. Fig. 1, 1st 10 measures only

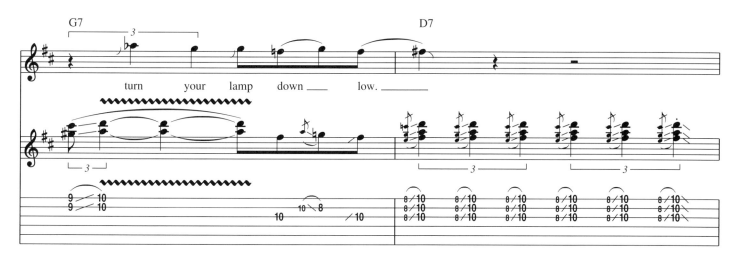

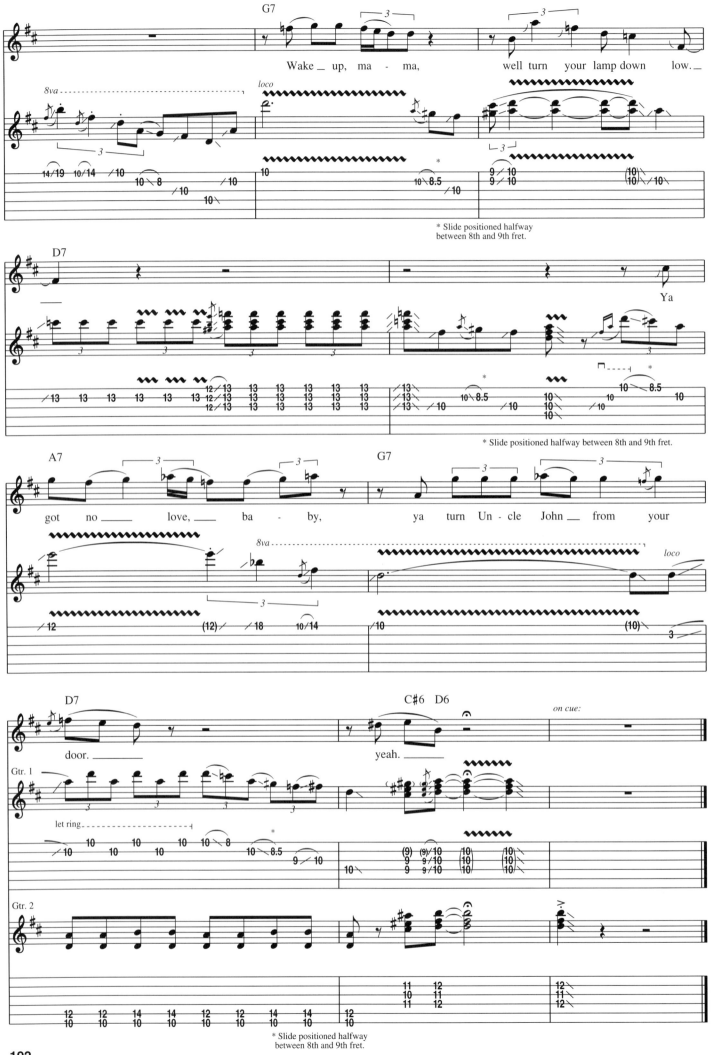

* Slide positioned halfway
between 8th and 9th fret.

* Slide positioned halfway between 8th and 9th fret.

* Slide positioned halfway
between 8th and 9th fret.

The Stumble

Words and Music by Freddie King and Sonny Thompson

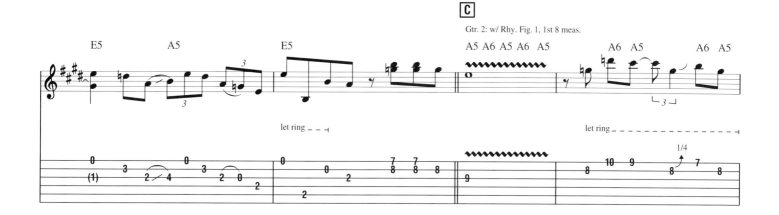

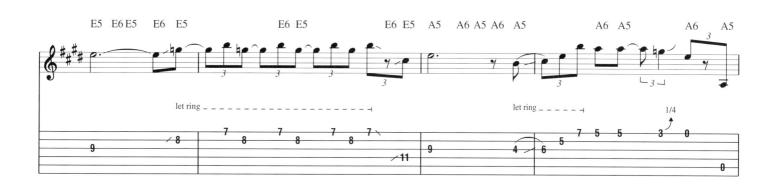

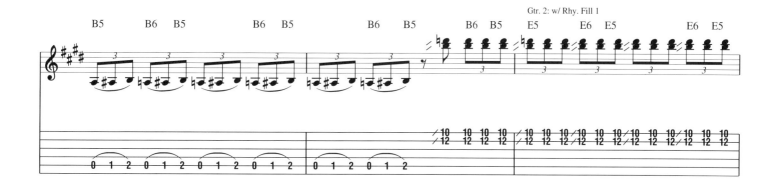

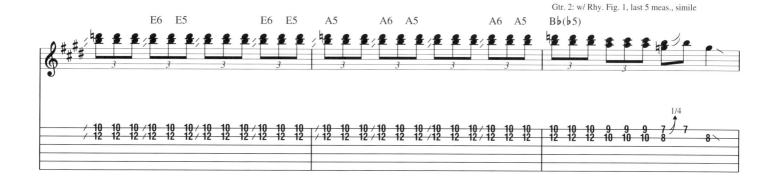

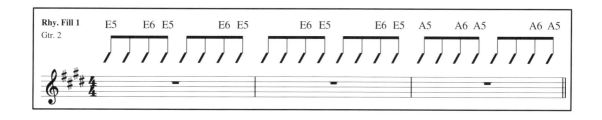

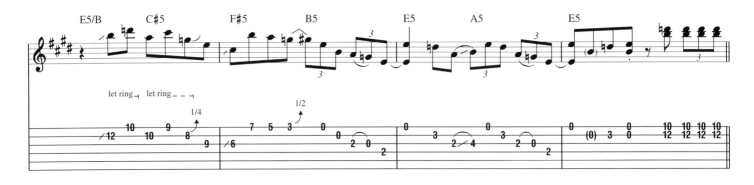

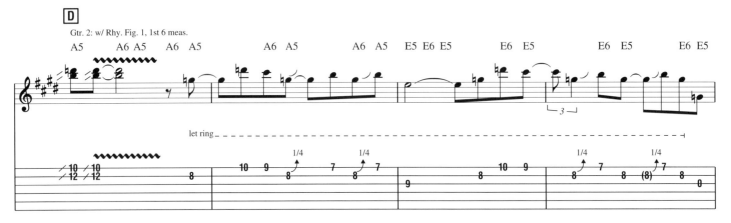

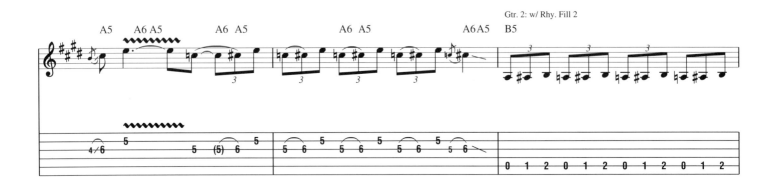

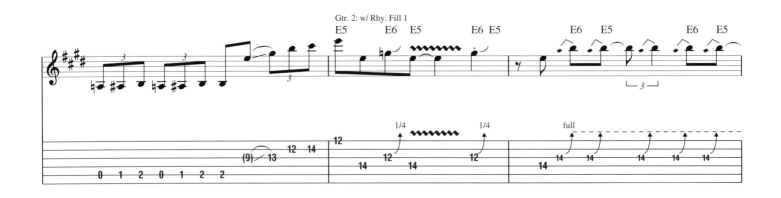

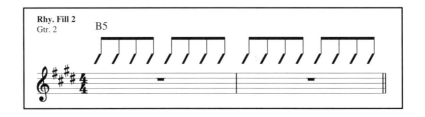

196

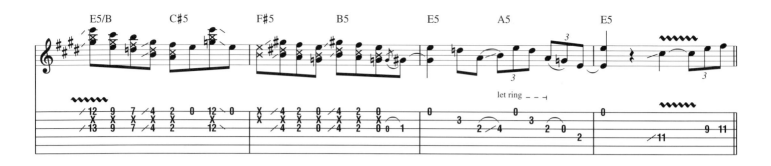

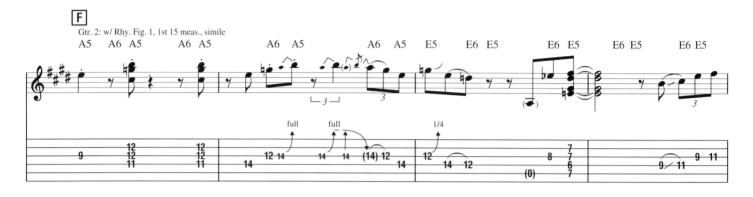

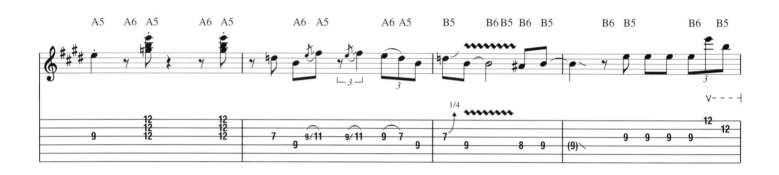

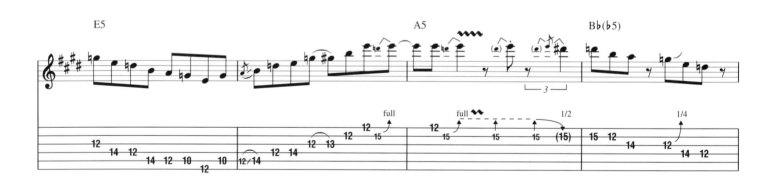

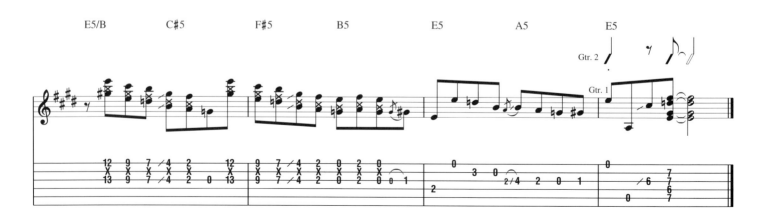

Sweet Little Angel

Words and Music by B.B. King and Jules Bihari

* Chord symbols reflect overall tonality.

T-Bone Shuffle

Words and Music by T-Bone Walker

*Chord symbols reflect overall tonality.

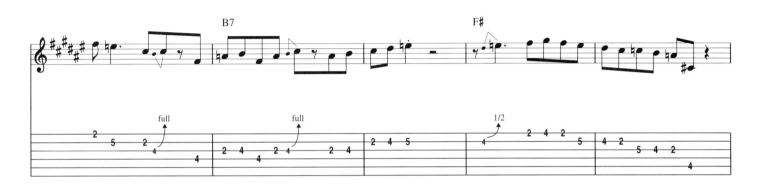

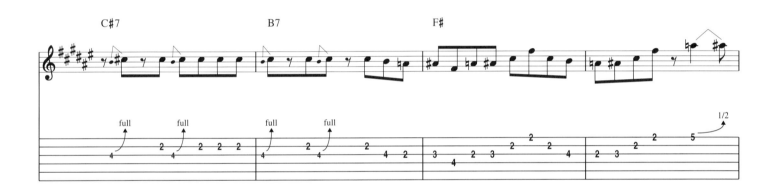

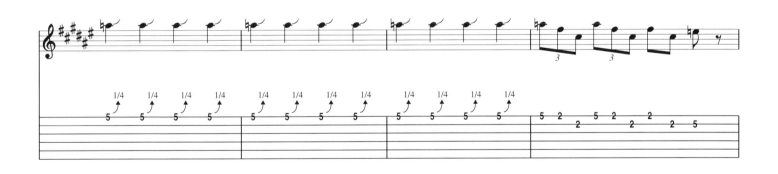

✛ *Coda 1*

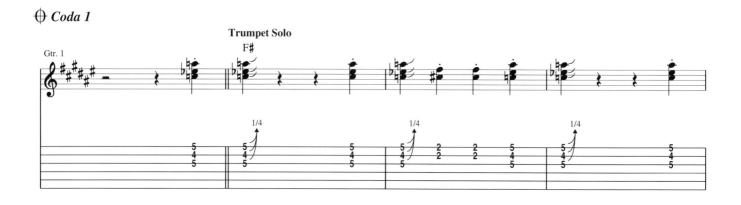

✛ *Coda 2*

The Things That I Used to Do

Words and Music by Eddie "Guitar Slim" Jones

* Symbols in parentheses represent chord names respective to capoed guitar. Symbols above reflect actual sounding chord.

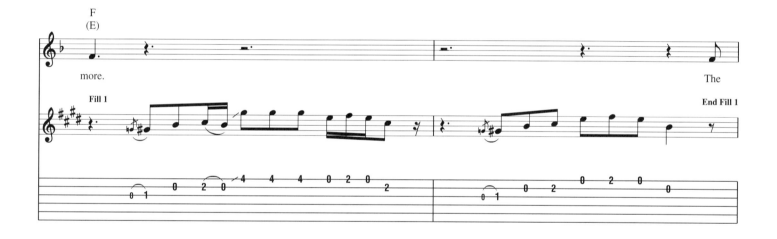

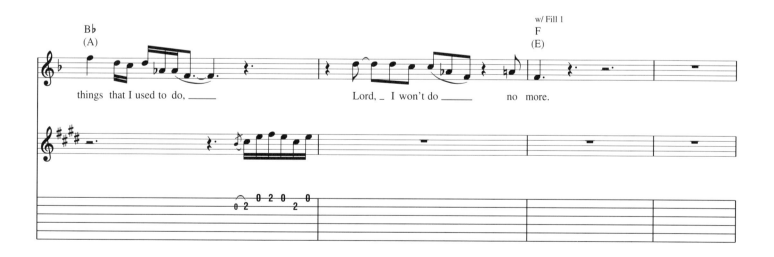

I used to set and hold your hand, ba - by, cry, ____ beg-gin' you not to go. ___

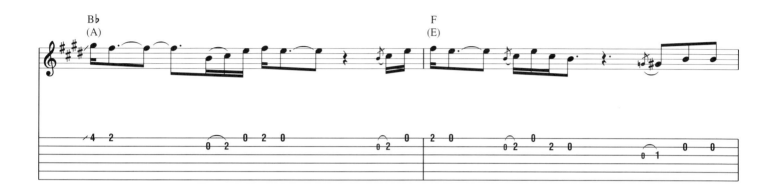

D.S. al Coda

I'm go-ing to send you back to your

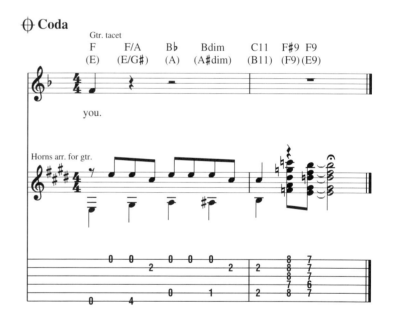

⊕ Coda

Gtr. tacet

F   F/A   Bb   Bdim   C11   F#9 F9
(E)   (E/G#) (A)   (A#dim) (B11) (F9)(E9)

you.

Horns arr. for gtr.

Additional Lyrics

2. I would search all night for you, baby,
   Lord, and my search would always end in vain.
   I would search all night for you, baby,
   Lord, and my search would always end in vain.
   But I knew all along, darlin',
   That you was hid out with your other man.

3. I'm going to send you back to your mother, baby,
   Lord, and I'm going back to my family too.
   I'm going to send you back to your mother, baby,
   Lord, and I'm going back to my family too.
   'Cause nothing I do that please you, baby,
   Lord, I just can't get along with you.

The Thrill Is Gone

Words and Music by Roy Hawkins and Rick Darnell

* Chord symbols reflect overall tonality.

Verse

1. The thrill is gone, __ the thrill is gone __ a-way.

The thrill is gone, ____ ba-by, the thrill is gone ____ a-way. ____

You know you done me wrong, _____ ba-by, and you'll __ be sor - ry some day. _____

Verse

2. The thrill is gone,   it's gone a - way _ from me. _____

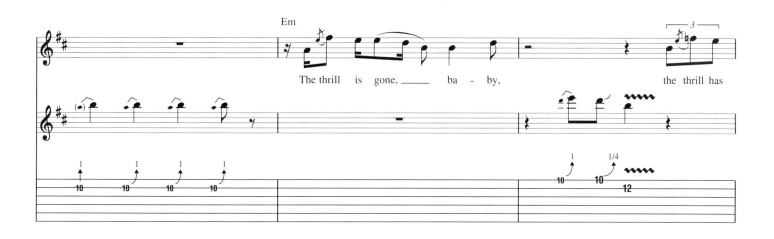

The thrill is gone, _____ ba - by,   the thrill has

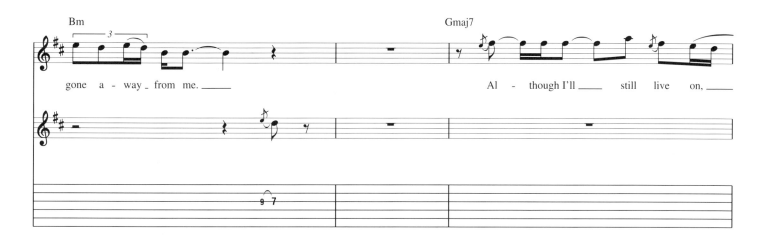

gone a - way _ from me. _____   Al - though I'll _____ still live on, _____

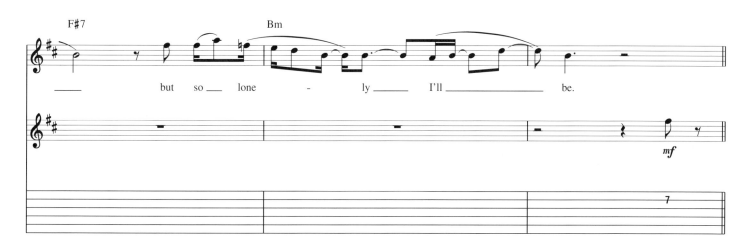

_____ but so lone   - ly _____ I'll _____ be.

Guitar Solo

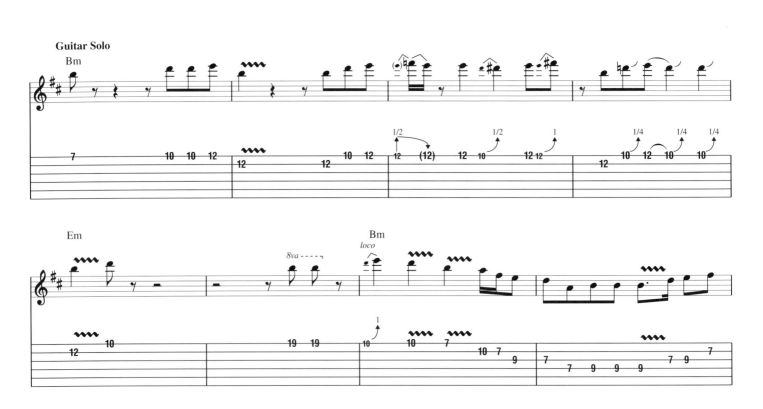

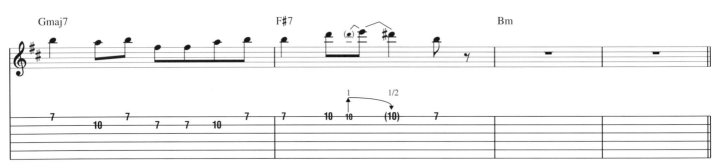

Verse

Gtr. 1 tacet

3. The thrill is gone, __ it's gone a-way __ for good. Oh,

the thrill is gone, _____ ba-by, it's gone _____ a-way for good.

Some-day I know I'll be hold-in' on, _____ ba-by, just like I know _____ a good man _____

Verse

should. 4. You know I'm __ free, free now, ____ ba - by,

Gtr. 1

I'm free _ from your _ spell. Whoa, I'm free _ free, free ____ now, I'm free __

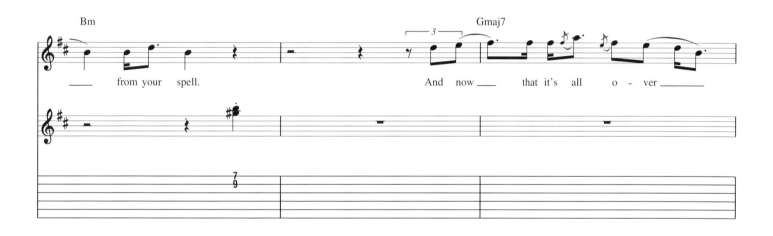

__ from your spell. And now ___ that it's all o - ver ____

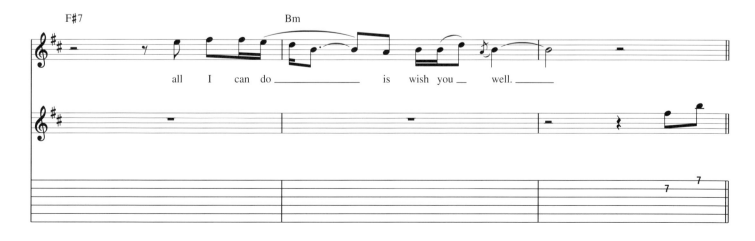

all I can do _____ is wish you _ well. ____

Outro-Guitar Solo

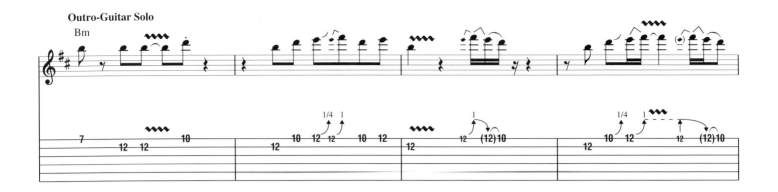

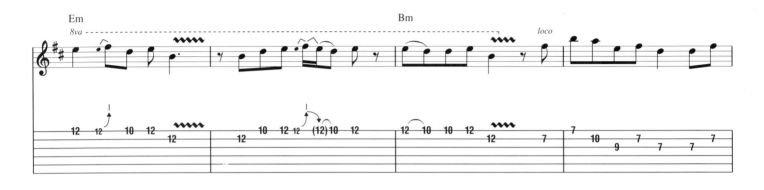

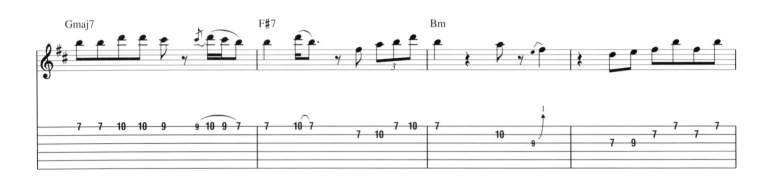

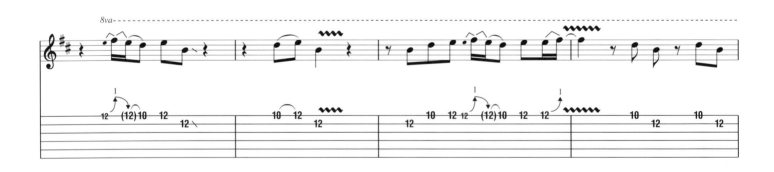

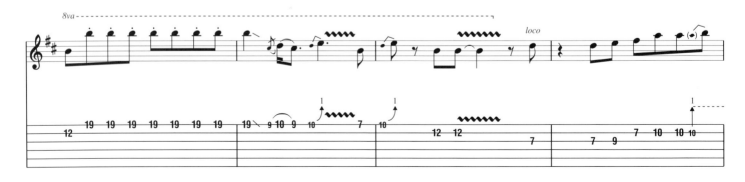

Wang Dang Doodle

Written by Willie Dixon

*Chord symbols reflect basic harmony.

Verse

1. Tell Au-to-mat-ic Slim, ___ tell Raz-or Tot-in' Jim. ___ Tell Butch-er Kneif Tot-in' An-nie, tell Fast Talk-in' Fan-nie. A,

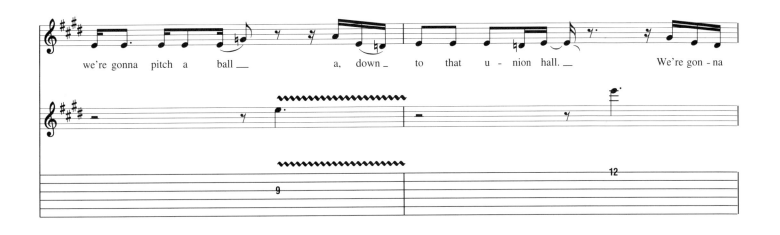

we're gonna pitch a ball ___ a, down ___ to that u - nion hall. ___ We're gon - na

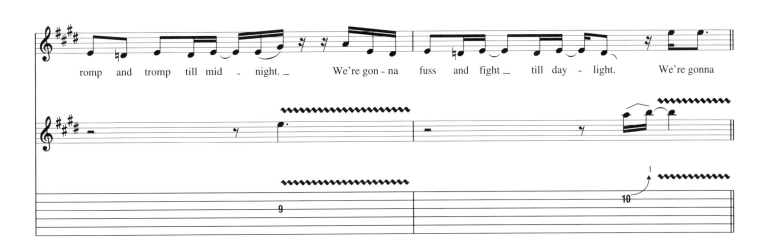

romp and tromp till mid - night. ___ We're gon - na fuss and fight ___ till day - light. We're gonna

Chorus

E7

pitch a wang ___ wang ___ doo - dle all night long, all ___ night long, all ___ night

Chorus

kick down all the doors. _ We're gon' pitch a wang wang doo-dle all _ night long, all __ night

long, _ all __ night long, _____ all __ night long, all ___ night

Guitar Solo

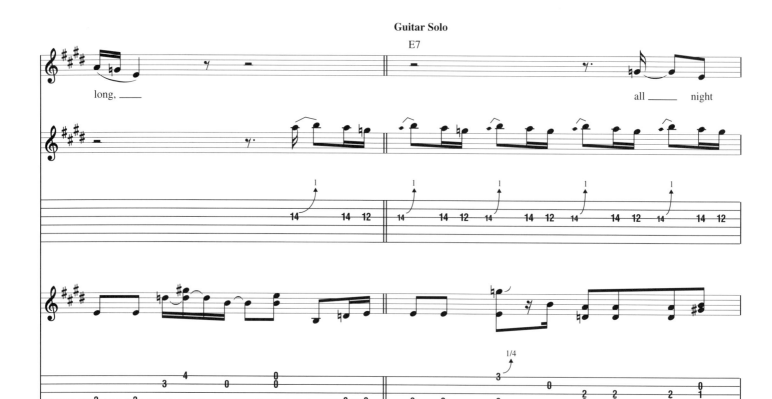

long, _____   all ___ night

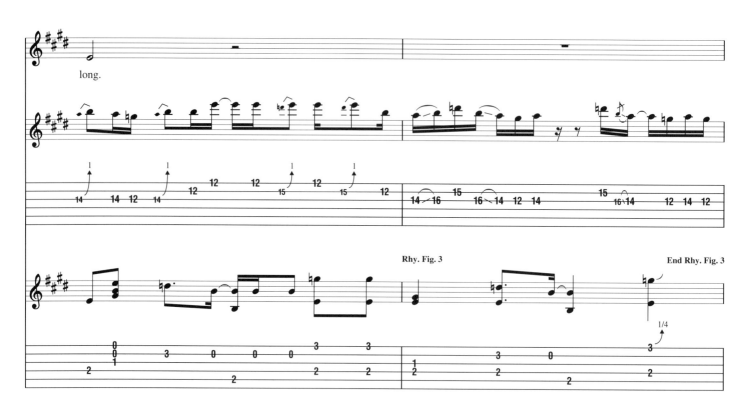

long.

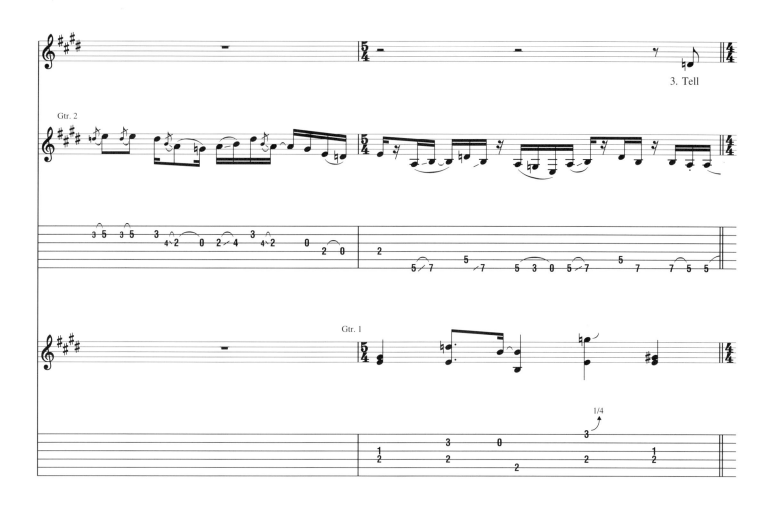

Verse

Fats, and Wash-board Sam, _ that ev-'ry-bod - y gon' jam. Tell Shak-in' Box - car Joe _ we got

saw - dust on the flo'. _ Tell Peg and Aunt Car-o-line Di _ we _ gon' to have a time. _ A, well, the

Outro-Chorus

E7

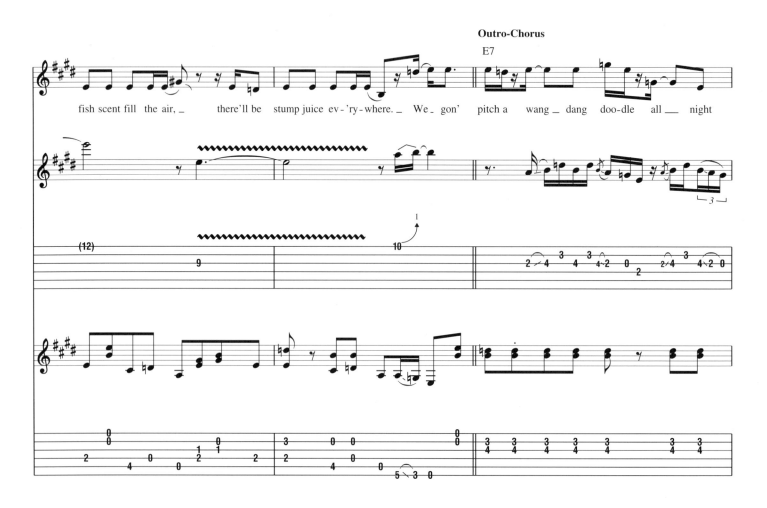

fish scent fill the air, _ there'll be stump juice ev-'ry-where. We _ gon' pitch a wang _ dang doo-dle all _ night

long, all ___ night long, all ___ night long, ___ all ___ night

long, all ___ night long, ___ all ___ night long, all ___ night

Begin fade *Fade out*

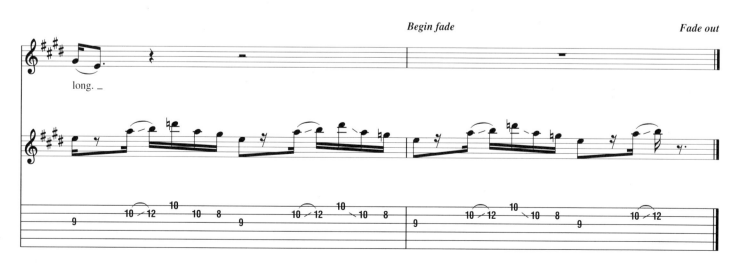

long. __

Guitar Notation Legend

Guitar Music can be notated three different ways: on a *musical staff*, in *tablature*, and in *rhythm slashes*.

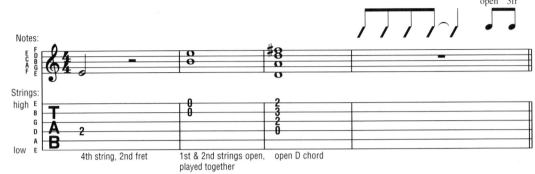

RHYTHM SLASHES are written above the staff. Strum chords in the rhythm indicated. Use the chord diagrams found at the top of the first page of the transcription for the appropriate chord voicings. Round noteheads indicate single notes.

THE MUSICAL STAFF shows pitches and rhythms and is divided by bar lines into measures. Pitches are named after the first seven letters of the alphabet.

TABLATURE graphically represents the guitar fingerboard. Each horizontal line represents a string, and each number represents a fret.

4th string, 2nd fret   1st & 2nd strings open, played together   open D chord

---

HALF-STEP BEND: Strike the note and bend up 1/2 step.

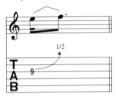

BEND AND RELEASE: Strike the note and bend up as indicated, then release back to the original note. Only the first note is struck.

HAMMER-ON: Strike the first (lower) note with one finger, then sound the higher note (on the same string) with another finger by fretting it without picking.

TRILL: Very rapidly alternate between the notes indicated by continuously hammering on and pulling off.

PICK SCRAPE: The edge of the pick is rubbed down (or up) the string, producing a scratchy sound.

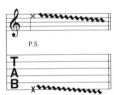

TREMOLO PICKING: The note is picked as rapidly and continuously as possible.

WHOLE-STEP BEND: Strike the note and bend up one step.

PRE-BEND: Bend the note as indicated, then strike it.

PULL-OFF: Place both fingers on the notes to be sounded. Strike the first note and without picking, pull the finger off to sound the second (lower) note.

TAPPING: Hammer ("tap") the fret indicated with the pick-hand index or middle finger and pull off to the note fretted by the fret hand.

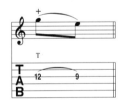

MUFFLED STRINGS: A percussive sound is produced by laying the fret hand across the string(s) without depressing, and striking them with the pick hand.

VIBRATO BAR DIVE AND RETURN: The pitch of the note or chord is dropped a specified number of steps (in rhythm) then returned to the original pitch.

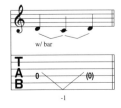

GRACE NOTE BEND: Strike the note and immediately bend up as indicated.

VIBRATO: The string is vibrated by rapidly bending and releasing the note with the fretting hand.

LEGATO SLIDE: Strike the first note and then slide the same fret-hand finger up or down to the second note. The second note is not struck.

NATURAL HARMONIC: Strike the note while the fret-hand lightly touches the string directly over the fret indicated.

PALM MUTING: The note is partially muted by the pick hand lightly touching the string(s) just before the bridge.

VIBRATO BAR SCOOP: Depress the bar just before striking the note, then quickly release the bar.

SLIGHT (MICROTONE) BEND: Strike the note and bend up 1/4 step.

WIDE VIBRATO: The pitch is varied to a greater degree by vibrating with the fretting hand.

SHIFT SLIDE: Same as legato slide, except the second note is struck.

PINCH HARMONIC: The note is fretted normally and a harmonic is produced by adding the edge of the thumb or the tip of the index finger of the pick hand to the normal pick attack.

RAKE: Drag the pick across the strings indicated with a single motion.

VIBRATO BAR DIP: Strike the note and then immediately drop a specified number of steps, then release back to the original pitch.